THE SACRED STONE CIRCLES *of* STANTON DREW

Gordon Strong

First published in Great Britain in 2012 by Skylight Press,
210 Brooklyn Road, Cheltenham, Glos GL51 8EA

Designed and typeset by Rebsie Fairholm
Publisher: Daniel Staniforth
Photography by Rebsie Fairholm
Back cover painting by Gordon Strong

The author and publisher would like to thank the Reference Library staff at Bristol Central Library for their kind assistance in sourcing illustrations.

www.skylightpress.co.uk

Printed and bound in Great Britain by Lightning Source, Milton Keynes
Typeset in Adobe Caslon Pro. Titles set in Yana, a font by Laura Worthington and Newcomen, a font from Insigne Design.

British Library Cataloguing in Publication Data.
A catalogue record for this book is available from the British Library.

ISBN 978-1-908011-58-9

The stones are great
And magic power they have.

Layamon – 12th Century Chronicler.

The way to approach a puzzle is to think about it for a while, look at all the facts you can find out about it, and then take a guess.

Kary Mullis

'...When the Common Market comes to Stanton Drew.'

Adge Cutler and the Wurzels

THE COVE

STONES IN MIDDLE HAM

VIEW OF N.E. CIRCLE, LOOKING W.

3305 feet from Stones in Middle Ham to centre of Great Circle

PLAN

OF THE

ANCIENT REMAINS

AT

STANTON DREW,

SOMERSET.

SURVEYED IN 1872 AND 1876.

REVISED IN 1894.

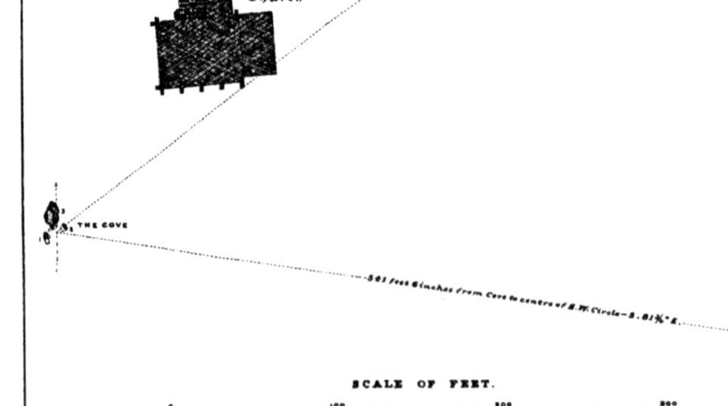

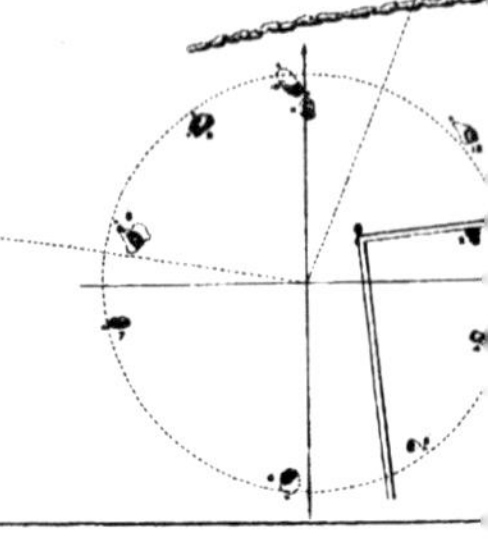

SCALE OF FEET.

0 100 200 300

C. W. Dymond, F.S.A., delt. August, 1894.

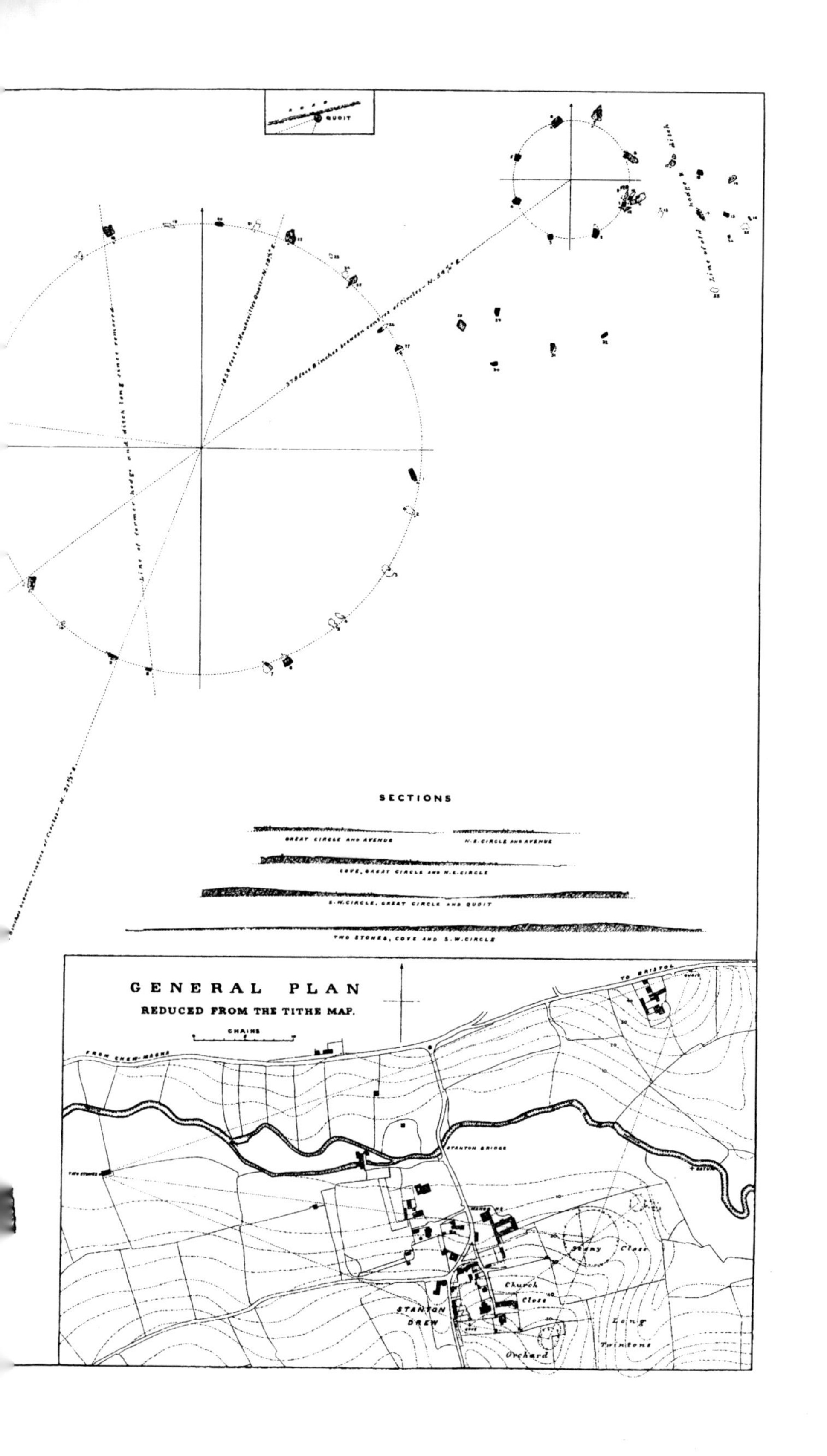
ROAD
QUOIT
Line of old hedge & ditch
Line of former hedge and ditch long since removed
1856 feet to Hautville's Quoit—N. 19¾° E.
378 feet 8 inches between centres of Circles—N. 54¾° E.
SECTIONS
GREAT CIRCLE AND AVENUE
N.E. CIRCLE AND AVENUE
COVE, GREAT CIRCLE AND N.E. CIRCLE
S.W. CIRCLE, GREAT CIRCLE AND QUOIT
TWO STONES, COVE AND S.W. CIRCLE
GENERAL PLAN
REDUCED FROM THE TITHE MAP.
CHAINS
FROM CHEW-MAGNA
TO BRISTOL
QUOIT
STANTON BRIDGE
TWO STONES
STANTON DREW
Stony Close
Church Close
Long Twintons
Orchard

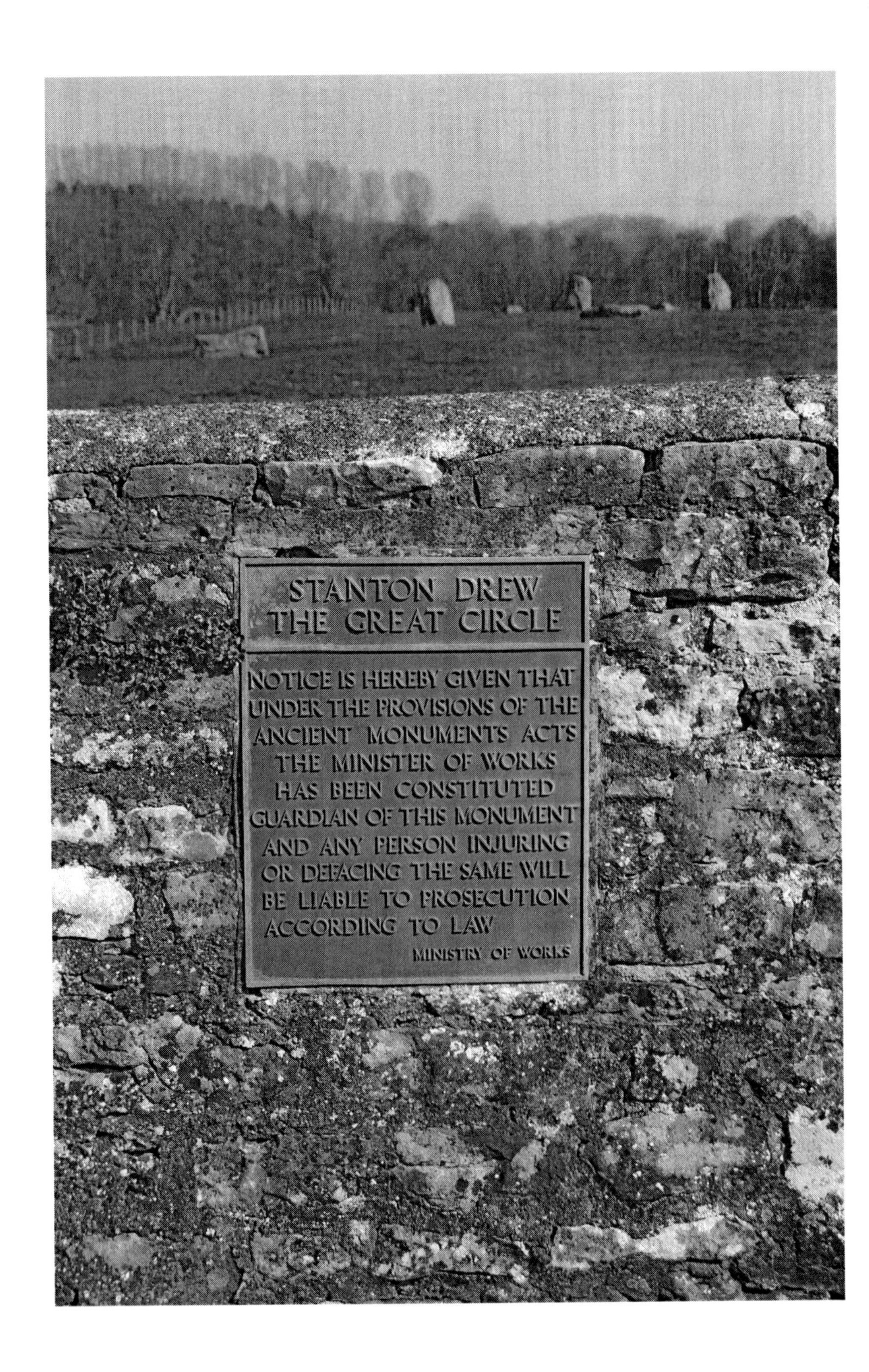
STANTON DREW
THE GREAT CIRCLE
NOTICE IS HEREBY GIVEN THAT
UNDER THE PROVISIONS OF THE
ANCIENT MONUMENTS ACTS
THE MINISTER OF WORKS
HAS BEEN CONSTITUTED
GUARDIAN OF THIS MONUMENT
AND ANY PERSON INJURING
OR DEFACING THE SAME WILL
BE LIABLE TO PROSECUTION
ACCORDING TO LAW
MINISTRY OF WORKS

Contents

Foreword 9
Acknowledgements 11
Introduction 13
What are Stone Circles? 15
The Woodhenge 25
Antiquarians and Analogies 31
Serpents, Dragons and the Sun 37
The Watery Moon 45
The Venus Cycle 55
Comets and Energy Lines 61
Sacrificing the King 67
A Holographic Universe? 73
The Otherworld 83
The Eternal Waters 87
A Continuing Magic 91
Bibliography 97

Foreword

I am amazed that I wrote most of what follows nearly ten years ago. I have revised the text and added a lot of new insights and information but the rest still stands, as do thankfully the stones at Stanton Drew.

A lot of people, even those who live relatively close to the stone circles, don't know of their existence and maybe that's how it should be. Stanton Drew is a secret place, one that has built up its magical power over thousands of years. Those who embrace it are probably guided there by the spirits of our Neolithic ancestors.

My original foreword ended with these words, 'I have learned much about this wondrous place over the years and now the shadows have faded, the figures in the landscape move and have their own being.' I'll stick with that.

Gordon Strong

Portishead, UK
February 2012

Acknowledgements

It would be almost impossible to list all the people who have given me knowledge and insights about Stanton Drew over the years. I originally described them as being 'from bikers to Buddhists', which covers a pretty wide spectrum. Some I met at the stones became close friends; others have drifted away to all corners of the cosmos.

I began my researches with the existing surveys of the site made by local archaeologists Dr. Boycott and Marian Benham. Reg Jackson, then of the Bristol Museum, vetted and approved my first efforts. Marian Green suggested I should take part in the Druid celebrations on the Quarter days at Stanton Drew. There I met Prof. Ronald Hutton and many a druid, including Adrian Rooke and Colin Irving. Mediums Ian and Norma Parfitt and Rob Dumbarton recorded their impressions, on an evening when the sky was lit with lightning and the heavens rocked with storms.

Sig Lonegren, Nicholas Mann and myself hosted many a tour of the site. Authors Peter Marshall, Alan Richardson and C.J.Stone all provided material I could abundantly quote. Geoff Ward interviewed me about the nature of Stanton Drew and wrote a very insightful piece for the Western Daily Press. Adam Stout had some useful things to say about the face of archaeology.

English Heritage owns the stones at Stanton Drew, but the farmer Richard Young is the owner of the field in which the Circles stand. No one could imagine a more generous and understanding man. Man of Avalon Palden Jenkins awarded me the title of 'Champion of Stanton Drew' – an honour I hope I can still live up to. Robin Heath, as well as introducing me to the complexities of archaeoastronomy, guided me to Alexander Thom's survey of the site.

Victoria Brudal, someone I have journeyed with in many lifetimes, helped with the original manuscript. Etymology, proofreading and perceptions were willingly offered by her. Tenjo, I thank for simply being there when it mattered. Julie in Bristol Central Library suggested the quote from Adge Cutler, a Somerset figure in his own way as legendary as the stone circles.

I'm grateful to Basil Wilby, a great inspiration in countless ways over the years, for giving me the opportunity to publish this book. Daniel Staniforth and Rebsie Fairholm have faultlessly guided this project from its inception, and constantly ensuring that it was a delight for me to be involved. Rebsie's photographs also add a visionary dimension, perfectly reflecting the ambiance of this marvellous place.

Gordon Strong
Portishead, February 2012

Introduction

On Beltane 2011 I took a new acquaintance to Stanton Drew for the first time. As we approached the NE Circle she enquired, quite innocently, 'Does it always look like this?' I stared in amazement at what was before us – the whole of the area inside the circle was covered with glowing, yellow flowers. Alone, we held hands, standing in the heart of the sun, and looking out between the two stone pillars into the West. We still talk about that moment together, when we had spontaneously evoked magic. Stanton Drew is one of the best places to do that kind of thing.

All sorts of people have had all sorts of experiences at Stanton Drew, some of them not so positive. I have heard of those who would not even enter Stoney Close, the field where the stones are situated. Others have been overwhelmed by the 'energies' there. I try to keep an open mind as I have experienced quite a lot extraordinary phenomena in my life. Alan Richardson in his book *Spirits of the Stones*[1] mentions not infrequent accounts of dark, potent forces at sacred sites, some dangerous and malevolent.

Some visitors to megalithic (Gk. *megas*, big; *lithos*, stone) monuments have strong physical reactions, amounting to nausea, headaches and dizziness. It is interesting that more renowned sites such as the Pyramids, Chartres Cathedral or Ayers Rock, having almost built-in expectations, do not evoke this reaction. Many stone circles or long barrows are in obscure locations and are often unprepossessing in appearance – they are not 'tourist attractions'.

It should be kept in mind when visiting a site such as Stanton Drew that its purpose, as well as a place of meeting, celebration, and commerce even, was to enter another world. A consecrated space it is, and is there to enhance the possibility of contacting the non-physical, the non-rational. In pagan times, no conscious division between spiritual and 'ordinary' consciousness would have been recognised.

---

1 Alan Richardson, *Spirits of the Stones: Visions of Sacred Britain* (London: Virgin Publishing 2001)

To the ancients, magic was considered to be a practical tool, a means to an end. Providing successful hunting, and rain for crops, this was the business of the wizard. His practice or methods had no overtones of 'good' or 'evil'; such an interpretation would become part of the Christian belief that followed. When this new religion came to prominence, its eventual *raison d'être* was to eradicate all pantheistic beliefs. It should not be forgotten that, in the 11th Century, the Emperor Charlemagne converted most of Europe at the point of a sword.

Over the centuries our ancient heritage has been variously abused, derided and treated with indifference. We are fortunate to live in an age that has rediscovered its respect for what went before and, at last, there is a growing respect for the wisdom of our ancestors. Neolithic monuments are now preserved for all, and we have the privilege of exploring them.

And how should the visitor act when they approach Stanton Drew, or indeed any other 'sacred site'? First, enter from the East, the place of the magician. Then turn off your thoughts, and experience! Take off your shoes and feel the good earth under your feet! Listen to the songs of the wildlife around, tune in to the Great Goddess in her wondrous and bountiful beauty! Most important of all, speak with the stones, listen to what they have to say to you, and remember it.

1

What are Stone Circles?

ROCK IS THE body of the Earth and stones are its skeleton. From early times, mountains and high places were exalted, and the practice of erecting stone monuments occurs throughout much of the world. From the Pyramids to tombstones and altars, stone has been a significant material for man. It is heavy, requires a great amount of energy to move around, but is eminently resilient. Stone is permanent in a way that humans are not, and it is somehow reassuring to know that the stones of Stanton Drew will still be there a long time after we have departed to, hopefully, greater things.

The nature of stone for man could be seen as twofold, defensive and aggressive at the same time. A stone-axe is a weapon, a cave is a shelter. The associations become more profound when we consider a stone circle. There is both a sense of belonging created by the space within, and a feeling of being separated from the world outside. Great power resides in stone circles as we shall discover. They may be a womb, a temple, or a portal into the next world.

The term *stone circle* refers to a type of megalithic monument found in many parts of the world. Of those that exist in the British Isles the archaeologist Jean-Pierre Mohan writes,

> British Isles megalithism is outstanding in the abundance of standing stones, and the variety of circular architectural complexes of which they formed a part...strikingly original, they have no equivalent elsewhere in Europe – strongly supporting the argument that the builders were independent.[2]

The precise function of stone circles will always be open to debate. All we can say with any certainty is that their purpose was intimately connected with the beliefs of the prehistoric people who built them. Their orientation may be on sight lines with the sun or the moon, or

---

2 Jean Pierre Mohan, *Les Monde de Megalithes* (Tournai: Casterman 1989) p.65

they may be not. Sites such as Stanton Drew were regarded as sacred long before any attempt to construct any monument there. As Sig Lonegren tells us,

> Until the beginning of the Neolithic period, roughly 4000 BC, Europeans were hunter-gatherers. As we followed the herds and the various crops that ripened in their time, we were in tune with Nature, and were naturally at the appropriate centres at the specific time of the year...[3]

The construction of stone circles began circa 3700 BC and continued for over two thousand years. At the end of that period it seems that new beliefs did not necessitate the building of such monuments. The most accurate date we have for the construction of the first monuments at Stanton Drew is 2500 BC. It seems obvious that the site came first, in that the intrinsic 'feel' indicated where the monument should be. The land determines its own temples, for Nature is wiser than man.

In attempting to find the 'purpose' of Stanton Drew or any megalithic monument we must first attempt to understand the way our Neolithic ancestors thought. As Peter Marshall explains,

> The megaliths went up when humans first settled down. Their building coincided with the momentous shifts from nomadic hunter-gathering to farming crops and herding animals. ... there was a surplus of food, and sufficient leisure to enable people to engage in great collective works of building and engineering, art and architecture.[4]

Although often incomplete, stone circles still remain an intrinsic part of the landscape, a potent reminder of an ancient culture. In the twenty-first century we should mark the industry and wisdom and of those who built such monuments. The enthusiasm and the motive for continuing such a huge undertaking would need to have been sustained through several generations.

Apart from simple sweat and true grit, the method of erecting the stones at Stanton Drew has been the subject of some abstruse speculation. The use of sound to raise stones is one explanation that has been offered. A fourteenth century illustration shows Merlin

---

3 Sig Lonegren, *Spiritual Dowsing* (Glastonbury: Gothic Image 1986) p.23

4 Peter Marshall, *Europe's Lost Civilization* (London: Hodder Headline 2006) p.4

constructing Stonehenge and it is a surreal image, with the wizard almost resembling a giant bricklayer. Is this a hint that the construction was completed without a hand being laid upon any of the huge blocks?

There are illustrated records of Tibetan monks raising huge boulders into the air by using the tones of trumpet-like instruments and the rhythmic sound of drums. Perhaps it is possible to tune into the energy of air and earth in order to achieve these things. As A.E.Huntley informs us, 'Primordial racial memories are brought to the surface more readily by music than by natural scenery or any other art'[5] which implies that the spirits of a place may also offer their aid to the task.

These ancient peoples would have enjoyed a temperate climate, one milder than the conditions we encounter at present. Their dwellings would have been functional and no trace of these has survived, while their monuments are the legacy of an inspired people, committed totally to the ethos they evolved over generations.

With the arrival of the Beaker Folk circa 2000 BC, a waning of any devotion around megalithic monuments begins. These new arrivals had no use for stone circles and were more concerned with constructing round barrows to honour their heroes. Chieftains were interred with grave goods, much gold and the trappings of power displayed with them. It is tempting to attribute the advent of this trend to the ascent of a warrior, male energy to displace that of the Goddess. The Age of Aries began at this time, displacing the Age of Taurus and continuing until the Birth of Christ, one that ushered in the Age of Pisces.

The most rewarding route to approach Stanton Drew is from the north, taking in Dundry Hill and Maes Knoll, an Iron Age fort. Many old place names in Somerset have a Gaelic origin, *Maes* Knoll being one example. Of Welsh origin, the word simply means 'field', a reference to the wide escarpment that makes up most of this encampment. Another derivation of Maes may be from *Merces*, a border, and this may refer to the area once being enclosed. Maes Knoll Tump predates the earth wall of the fort. This marks the beginning of West Wansdyke, named by the Anglo-Saxons after their god Woden. This deep ditch

5 A.E. Huntley, *The Divine Proportion* (New York: Dover, 1970)

was constructed in the 7th Century to denote the border with territory held by the Romano-Celts, or 'Britons' as they originally were.

The term 'fort' may be a misnomer as it is often difficult to reconcile the tactical advantage of these Iron-Age sites with their position. Maes Knoll is a good example: it has one earth wall, which admittedly would be difficult to surmount, but the land beyond simply slopes gently away from it. It is often a more rewarding approach to surmise that many places on high ground were settlements rather than military outposts.

The borders of the kingdom of Wales once extended much further to the east and south than the present day, and a great number of megalithic monuments are to be found in this area. The Anglo-Saxon invaders drove the Britons northwards out of Somerset, westwards out of Wiltshire and south into Cornwall. This exodus brought about the annexation of the Celtic kingdoms from the country that was to become *Angle land* or England. From the Anglo-Saxon name *Stantune* 'homestead of the stones', the name Stanton Drew is derived.

In the Middle Ages the land surrounding the stone circles was owned by the Drogo family, thus the derivation *Drew of Stone Town*. Castle Drogo on Dartmoor, the location of many a dolmen, is a modern construction (1910) although built on land owned by a Norman Baron, Drogo de Teign. A tenuous correspondence exists here between *draig* and dragon.

The winding road through Norton Malreward joins the B3130 and from the humpbacked bridge, which crosses the River Chew at the edge of the village, two of the three stone circles can be seen quite clearly. The largest of these, known as the Great Circle, has a diameter of 112m and encloses an area of 2000 square metres, exceeding the dimensions of Stonehenge. As with the Northeast (NE) Circle (diameter 29.5m), it was approached by an avenue of standing stones.

The size of the stone version of the Great Circle would have been determined by the dimensions of the previous 'woodhenge', a structure which will be discussed later. It is possible that the builders of the stone circles were frustrated by lack of space when they came to erect the NE Circle, the river being probably much wider then. At the northern edge of the site the ground slopes markedly also, so the position of the NE circle and its close proximity to the Great Circle was thus inevitable.

Part of the Great Circle, looking east towards the NE Circle.

The Great Circle. The undulation in ground level is the line of an old hedge and ditch which formerly divided the site.

The alignment of the site to the north appears deliberate. Kenneth Meadows explains the significance of this orientation:

> North is considered to be the direction of refreshment and renewal, and the reception of knowledge and wisdom ... in the seasonal cycle North is the direction of Winter when life appears to have withdrawn, but when there is activity in the seed beneath the surface ... it is considered to be the direction of mental activity[6] and of thoughts, ideas and creativity.[7]

The stones were probably quarried a few miles away, at Rudge Hill in West Harptree. As the largest of these has been estimated at weighing thirty tons, it is likely they were transported to where they now stand by raft, as the River Chew runs alongside the northern edge of the site. Marian Green once suggested to me that the stones were moved on sledges across frozen rivers during winter. It is possible; dramatic climatic changes certainly did occur around this period, and it is believed that a drought occurred in 3000 BC, severe enough to turn an area where cattle were once grazed into what is now known as the Sahara Desert. Marian also points out that extremes of weather might dramatically affect the behaviour of any prehistoric society, prompting its members to celebration in a warm climate and sacrifice in a hostile one.

Although many of the stones have fallen in the Great Circle, either pushed over or removed by the Quakers, it is still a most impressive feature. The Southwest circle has a diameter of 42m and is aligned to the Quoit and the Cove. Derived from Old English *cofa* an alcove, and from the ancient German for *hollow place*, this group of three stones (one split) stands in the garden of the Druids Arms some five hundred metres away. Tradition has a *shaman* occupying this sacred shelter in order to receive messages from the gods.

Apart from the fact that the stones of the Cove appear remarkably different from those of the circles, they are obviously much older. An interesting puzzle is to be found here, in that one stone lies flat between its two standing partners. Guy Underwood has this to say concerning such a formation:

---

6 The painter's studio always has a window in the North, as the purest and most consistent source of light comes from that direction.

7 Kenneth Meadows, *Shamanic Experience* (Dorset: Element Books 1991) p.144

> Their function appears to have been as directional signs for processions and other rituals. The supposition that all recumbent stones have fallen from an upright position is incorrect ... On the contrary, it is difficult to avoid the conclusion that the majority of these were cut to shape and placed in position by skilled diviners.[8]

I am more inclined to support this view than the suggestion by Bath and Camerton Archaeological Society that the Cove is the entrance to a long barrow. If this were so, its 'entrance' would face south; and this would not be impossible, but extremely unusual. Their survey of the Cove is part of a much larger project undertaken in 2009-10.[9] As an archaeological survey it is most thorough, but as so often with this 'scientific' approach, it lacks that degree of imagination that brings people like myself to Stanton Drew in the first place.

The Cove, in the garden of the Druids Arms pub.

Another isolated but equally significant feature is Hauteville's Quoit (*Quoit* may be *coit* – round or *quoin* corner). Hauteville (although literally *high place*) originates from the legend of *Hakewell*, a giant who, given Norton Manor by the villagers, and considering it a paltry offering, stood on Norton Hill and threw the stone to where it now

8 Guy Underwood, *The Pattern of the Past* (London: Sphere, 1972) p.68
9 This may be seen as a PDF file at www.baccas.org.uk.

lies. His adverse opinion of the gift is commemorated in the name of the village, *Norton Malreward.*

Another version of the tale, one slightly more prosaic, has Sir John Hauteville, a crusader, demonstrating to Edward I his displeasure with the gift of the Manor. What remains of the stone lies behind a hedge of Quoit Farm on the B3130 and it is not a very prepossessing sight. According to the Rev. John Collinson the original was supposed to have weighed thirty tons and stand 4m in height. This Victorian clergyman records that pieces of the Quoit were constantly being chipped off for road mending. Rodney Legg believes the stone to be a sarsen boulder from the Marlborough Downs which, to my mind, is as unlikely as Aubrey's suggestion that the stones for the circles came from St. Vincent Rocks at Clifton, Bristol.

In the eighteenth century, the antiquarian Stukeley mentioned the existence of a second quoit nearby, possibly near Chew Magna, but no trace remains of this. The Wimblestone, named after a *wimmel,* a mason's gimlet or perhaps the custom of *wimbling*, plaiting rope or corn sheaths together, and the flat megalith at Banwell, are two Somerset monuments that may also have links with the Stanton Drew circles. A dire warning about them still circulated in the locale in the 18th Century, as recorded by John Wood.

> No one, say the country people about Stanton Drew, was ever able to reckon the Number of the Metamorphosed Stones, or to take a draught of them, tho' several have attempted to do both, and proceeded until they were either struck dead upon the spot, or with such an illness as soon carried them off.[10]

There is a Welsh tradition that to destroy a standing stone will result in six generations of bad luck for the perpetrator of the crime. It is not known whether those who interfered with the stones at Stanton Drew, and various others nearby, suffered this fate.

A few old sources mention stones now missing from the original design. In the summer of 1664 Aubrey could not visit the site because of ripening corn, but nevertheless he observed that many of the stones (presumably from the Great Circle) had been removed by farmers

---

10 John Wood, *A Particular Description of Bath* Vol. I (1750)

desiring extra land. Burl even refers to two lost stones at East Harptree near to where we believe the megaliths originated.

Old maps of the 19th Century show *Tyning's Stones*, both nearly 2m in height. These were in a field called Middle Ham at Lower Tyning, to the north west of Hauteville's Quoit. In 1958 Pevsner mentions two stones that are likely to be the same and they seem to have disappeared shortly after. His description, 'dolomitic conglomerates ... sandstone ... jurassic limestone ... probably Dundry stone' appear to confirm they were the same makeup as the stones at the Stanton Drew circles. Local sources tell of these two megaliths, in a field adjoining Sandy Lane due West of the site. Apparently they were removed by persons known (or unknown) in the 1960s and never seen again.

The number of stones in each of the circles at Stanton Drew is obviously significant. At present, The Great Circle has thirty-two, the SW Circle twelve, and the NE Circle eight. These multiples of four seem significant, yet if very recent investigations at Stanton Drew are to be taken into account, this rather neat system is thrown into disarray.

The indefatigable dowser Paul M. Daw surveyed the South West circle in 2009 and mapped out the position of various stones he considered to be missing. His survey yielded a total of fifty-nine stones in the SW Circle! If this is correct a staggering number have been removed. More modest conclusions came to light when Daw plotted the position of nine missing stones in the two avenues leading to the NE Circle.

Just as interesting was his assertion in 2008 that there was a circle at nearby Chew Stoke in the graveyard of the Methodist Chapel. According to Daw the circle consisted of sixteen stones. This site may be the same as that reported by William Stukeley in the 1700s.

I was present when my good friend Joe Keaney, an American dowser from Oregon, surveyed the Stanton Drew site. He suggested the existence of an avenue, totalling thirty-eight stones, that led away from the NE Circle due east towards the River Chew. Joe also confirmed the possible position of the stones that were supposed to have once formed an aligned quadrilateral in the centre of the N.E. Circle. Evidence of this pattern was discovered during the 1997 Magnetometer Survey which revealed the existence of a woodhenge in the Great Circle. From these findings it may be concluded that at some time a smaller version of the present monument existed.

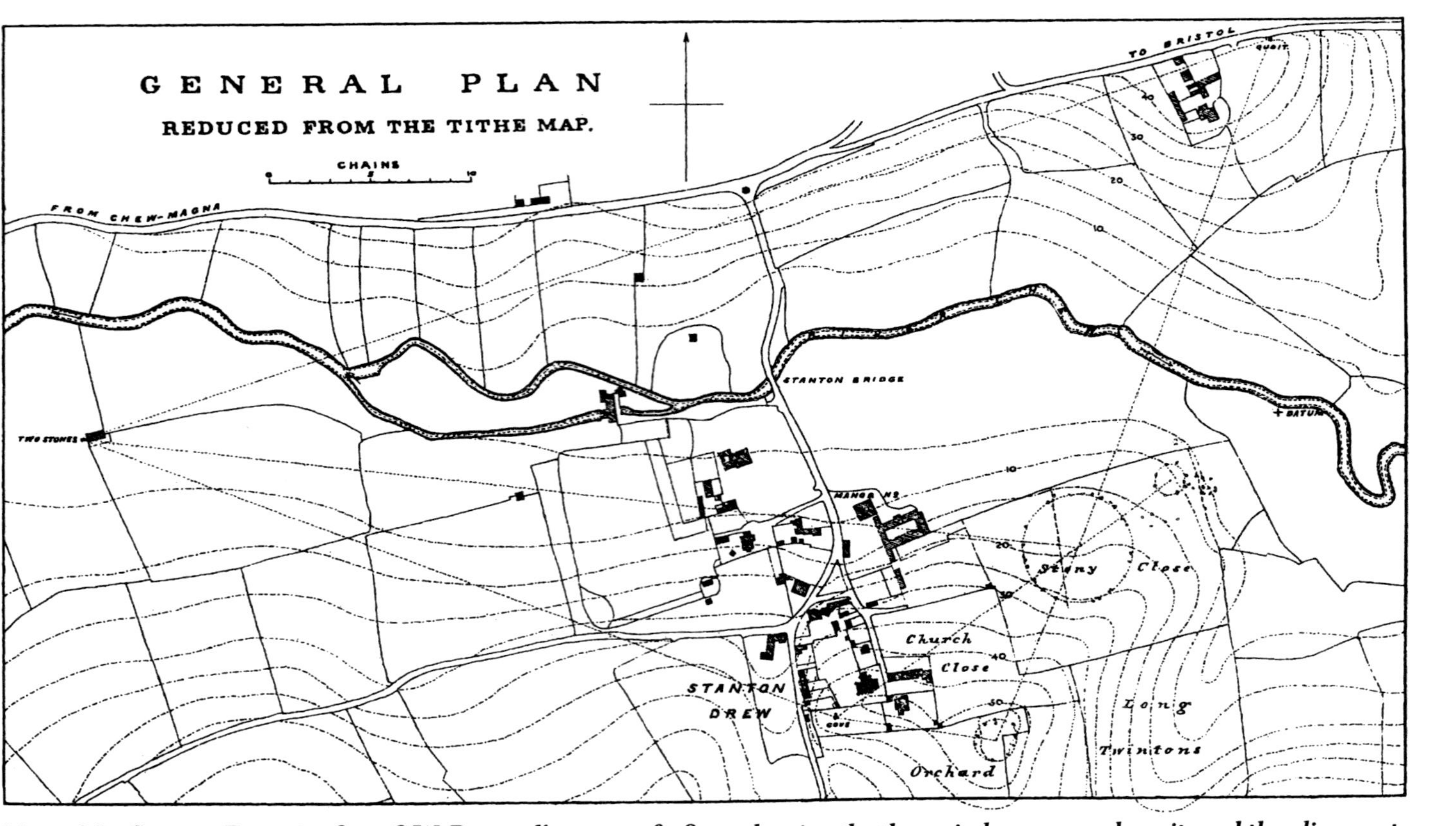

Map of the Stanton Drew site from C.W. Dymond's survey of 1894, showing the three circles, cove and quoit, and the alignments between them. Also shown are the 'Two Stones' to the west of the village, which have since been lost.

2

The Woodhenge

ARCHAEOLOGISTS define a henge as a bank made with the earth that is thrown up on to the outside edge when a ditch is dug. Mike Pitts describes a henge as an enclosed circular space, a definition that conveniently includes the many variations of design and materials used in their construction. More examples of henges are to be found in Britain than in Europe. If a line is traced through the centre of the British Isles from north to south, it will be seen that almost all henges and standing stones are to be found in the West.

The henge at Stanton Drew is thought to be older than Avebury or Stonehenge. Even with radio carbon dating, anomalies occur when attempting to establish an accurate date for any artefact. For the purposes of this study, parts of the Stanton Drew complex are assumed to date from 3500 BC. If this is correct the henge predates the Great Pyramid of Cheops in 2590 BC. Other events contemporaneous with its construction are the invention of the wheel in Mesopotamia, and the art of writing in Sumer.

Besides Stanton Drew, there are a few other *woodhenge* sites (or timber temples as some authorities quaintly refer to them) in Great Britain. Balfarg in Fife, Scotland is the most northerly, with Mount Pleasant in Dorset being the most southerly location. There are two sites at Durrington in Wiltshire, the more well-known Woodhenge consisting only of concrete markers, and others at Avebury and Stonehenge.

The only significant wooden construction in the eastern part of England is Seahenge, located near Norfolk. Undeniably an important artefact it may have been part of a chain of such monuments extending from the part of Europe that eventually became Germany, and across the area now covered by the North Sea. Some authorities, however, claim that the Seahenge monument dates from a later era as its construction appears to involve working with metal tools.

As Stanton Drew is rather a neglected site in terms of archaeological studies the existence of a woodhenge at Stanton Drew was not known until 1997. Conclusions about the site had been previously drawn from evidence gleaned from the stone circles. Thus it was realised that the stones of the Great Circle were later additions to a woodhenge at the site, eventually replacing it. The stone megaliths must have neatly filled the spaces between the hundreds of wooden posts and the ditch that made up the original construction.

The October 1997 *Caesium Gradiometer Survey* brought astonishing results. Comment at the time was fairly muted although this contemporary assessment, apparently an amalgam of two different sources, is reasonably forthright.

> The soil inside the Great Circle reveals that there were once 400-500 oak pillars on the site. These massive cylinders were probably a metre in diameter, 8 metres (26 feet) high, and weighed 5 tons each. The rings of pillars occupied an area about the size of a football field (100 metres in diameter). The Stanton Drew woodhenge was probably too large to have been roofed, but the oak columns might have been carved or decorated.[11]

The 1997 survey also revealed the existence of a henge ditch of diameter 135m and 7m wide surrounding the main circle and with an opening to the northeast. Geoffrey Wainwright had supervised the survey and details of his findings were given at a press conference convened in London. Reporters naturally asked the question *why*? What was the newly discovered woodhenge originally built for? Understandably, Wainwright, active at archaeological surveys since the 1950s, felt rather put on the spot. He knew that any response he made would become global news. Wisely perhaps, he settled for a middle-of-the-road view that it was '...used for ceremonies to ensure an adequate rainfall for crops...'

With the absence of any contemporary pictorial or written record, any view on the purpose of the installing of the woodhenge is as valid as any other. Most certainly the site was a gathering place for a catchment area that included Somerset, Gloucestershire and

---

11 Nigel Hawkes, 'Woodhenge Finds Rival Stone Circles', *The Times* (Nov. 11 1997). Another report may be found by Elizabeth Aveling, 'Magnetic Traces of a Giant Henge', *Nature*, (390:232, 1997)

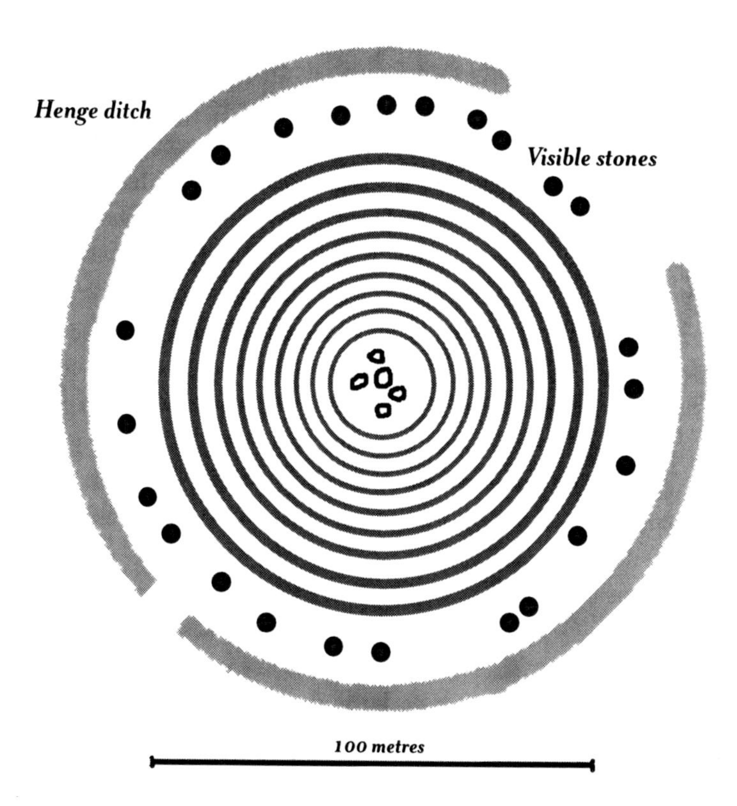

The magnetometer survey of the Great Circle by English Heritage in 1997 found evidence of nine concentric rings within the circle, indicating the site of an earlier woodhenge with an outer henge ditch. Some unidentified anomalies were also found in the centre of the circle.

probably parts of Wiltshire. It is in an ideal position, being relatively sheltered and having access by land and water. It can be assumed that the coming together of people would occur around the time when the first grass began to flourish and grazing was then made easier.

This time came to be known by the later Celts as Beltane, when beasts would be driven through the healing flames of fires. It cannot be assumed that the habits of Neolithic man were determined by a calendar established in a later era. Ancient pagan ceremonies were as likely to be determined by the vagaries of the English weather as anything else. Certainly the climate is not always kind in England in April or May, yet the proximity of wood for fuel and the lure of roasting meat would make any gathering at Stanton Drew attractive. Goods and gossip would be exchanged and the woodhenge could very well have been put to practical use in providing warmth and shelter.

Such a highly sophisticated structure with intricate lacing of timbers and lintels might have influenced the design of Stonehenge. It was obviously conceived and erected for some very significant purpose. The area covered is immense and could easily have accommodated a thousand people, if not more. A yew was felled here in 1962 and was perhaps a distant relative of the sacred wood that once stood on the site. Were the timber canopies of the woodhenge designed to create a forest-like effect? And again we ask why would such an enormous construction be sited at exactly this location? The question of 'power points' is commented on by Blanche Merz a Swiss geo-biologist,

> These ... can be defined as locations ... endowed with an energy, a force, and a strength. This quality is related to a precise geographical location which humans must have discovered in ancient times, whether by feeling, by intuition, by observation or by a deep knowledge of earth-cosmos relationships. ... In order to find these strong spots today we have to track down ... the ancient places of open-air worship...[12]

Most fascinating to speculate upon is the mindset of the woodhenge builders. Were deities first consulted about the design, even simple earth spirits? Were there 'project leaders' who then supervised the construction according to an established plan? Could there have been 'architects', 'bosses' and 'labourers'? Or were those who laboured upon this project so attuned that they had an intuitive understanding between each other? We know nothing of how our distant ancestors communicated with each other. Our own notions of language are tempered by ultra-sophisticated systems of transference of meaning. But as Steven Pinker explains,

> People know how to talk in more or less the sense that spiders know how to spin webs ... language is no more a cultural invention than is upright posture.[13]

---

12 Blanche Merz, *Points of Cosmic Energy* (1987)

13 Pinker, Steven, *The Language Instinct* (New York: Harper Perennial Library, 1995)

But in what form did they transmit or describe ideas with language? They must have used 'words of power', almost magical spells. And at the end of the day did they dance and sing or laugh heartily at the ways of the world? One likes to believe that they did, and gained as much joy as possible from their lives too.

It is also possible that an experienced team of woodhenge builders came to the site and directed the hauling of the massive timbers and setting of them in position. Probably only the leaders among them knew the real significance of the construction.[14] Highly organised lines of communication would have gathered the clans together for such projects, animals being herded there, crops gathered and provision made to feed all. It is likely that as the building progressed the woodhenge provided shelter for the workers and their families. Perhaps it became a covered structure shaped rather like a ring doughnut with a sacred space in the middle.

The noisy, animated scene would have continued for some months as the structure grew in size and complexity. Practical considerations must have determined the time of year chosen for building; perhaps work began in the Spring and finished at the Autumn Equinox. The completion of the project must undoubtedly have prompted great feasting and celebration.

14 The origins of Freemasonry may date from these times, in the sense of having an elite within the society possessing a secret knowledge of methods of construction.

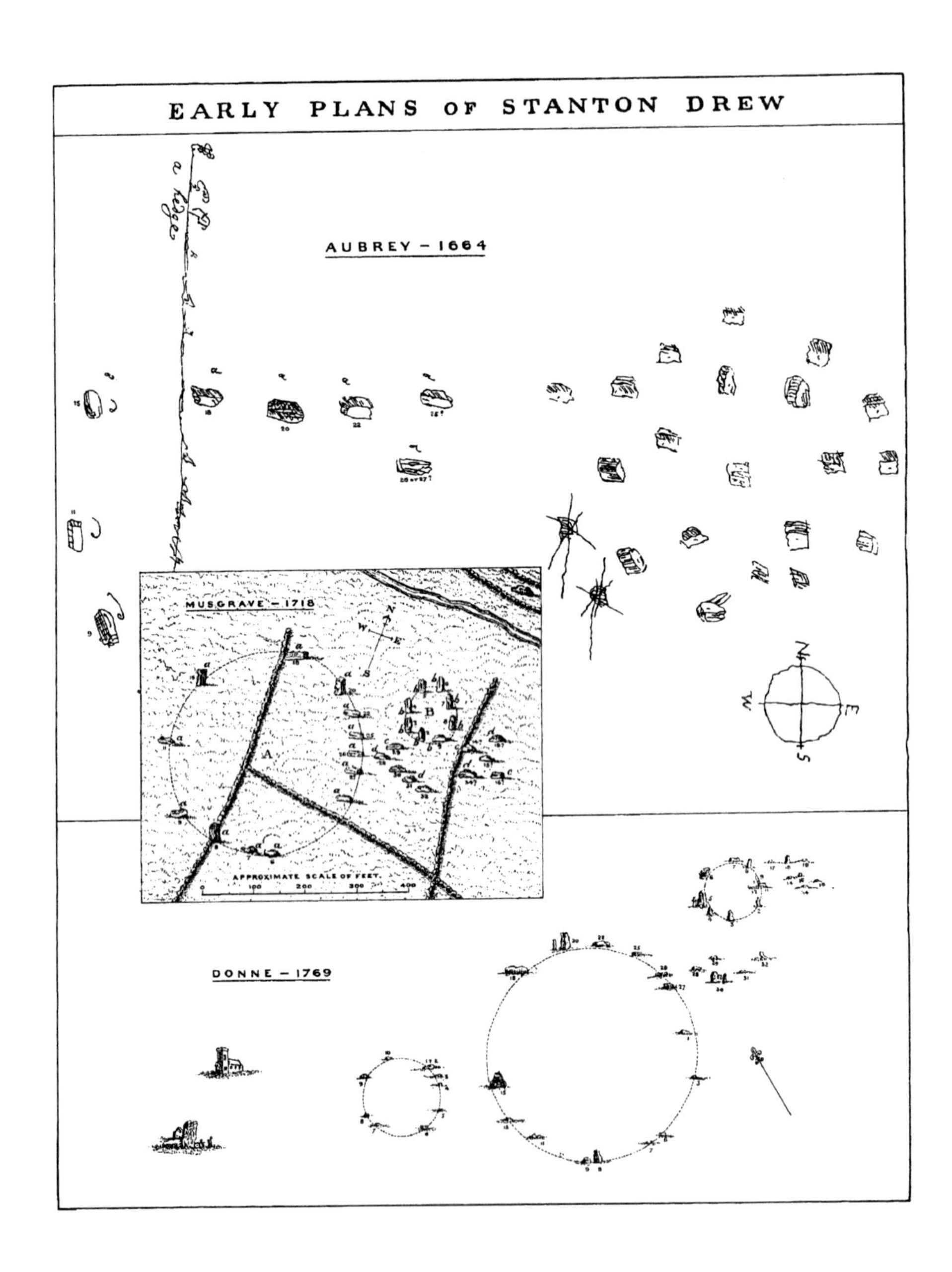
EARLY PLANS OF STANTON DREW
AUBREY – 1664
a hedge
MUSGRAVE – 1718
APPROXIMATE SCALE OF FEET.
0 100 200 300 400
DONNE – 1769

3

Antiquarians and Analogies

THE STONE CIRCLES at Stanton Drew were first noted by John Aubrey in 1664. Almost a century later a Mr. John Wood journeyed to Stanton Drew and made a plan of the site. His visit was followed by a storm and the villagers accused him of having 'Disturbed the Guardian Spirit of the metamorphosed stones.' In 1776 the first comprehensive drawings of the stones were made by William Stukeley. He believed that the site was part of a sacred pattern of landscape with centres at Stonehenge and Avebury.

Quite the most endearing of the antiquarian brotherhood is Ernest Sibree (1859-1927) who was lecturer in Oriental studies at the University of Bristol. His biographer considered it noteworthy to record that he married a Miss Kate Budgett and the union brought him 'a life of cloudless sky'. Sibree also took delight in listening to Welsh sermons, having a mastery of that language. His philological studies led him to a questionable conclusion, one based entirely on semantics. He maintained that the Anglo-Saxons had hauled fifty megaliths from the Mendips to Maes Knoll, where they were apparently guarded by the inhabitants of the fort, and then constructed the stone circles.

From his cosmological studies Sibree concluded that the purpose of Stanton Drew was as a *planetary calendar*, a much more plausible thesis. Aided by the research of Dymond[15], Sibree postulated that the stones were used to calculate the passing of a year. His thesis involves other stones as well as those in the three recognized circles. Those he wrote about, 'traces of which are observable in the circular course of the road passing through Upper Stanton Drew and in certain hedges bordering the fields to the west of the church' have since disappeared, if they actually existed at all.

It is not always possible to concur with Sibree, as the inclusion of extra features in the landscape seems to weaken any explanation of the

15 The unique description of the circles as *peristaliths* comes from Charles Dymond in 1896.

function of the site. He also holds the view that the stones represented a heptagramic planetary system used to record the passing of time. Days and months are assigned particular points on the circles with Venus and the Sun having prominent positions.

As has been already noted Sibree believed that the Anglo Saxons built the monument in honour of the goddess Frig, a deity corresponding with Venus. *Frig-Syl* means the pillar of Frig and the Pointer stone at Stonehenge is known as "Friars Heel" a corruption perhaps of *Fri-Sil.* A conjunction of the Sun with Friars Heel (or Venus) at Midsummer may represent a symbolic marriage between Heaven and Earth, the length of a solar year being fixed by the interval between the rising of Venus on consecutive midsummer days. It is not easy to follow Sibree's system but for those who wish to attempt the task a diagram is reproduced in his published work.[16]

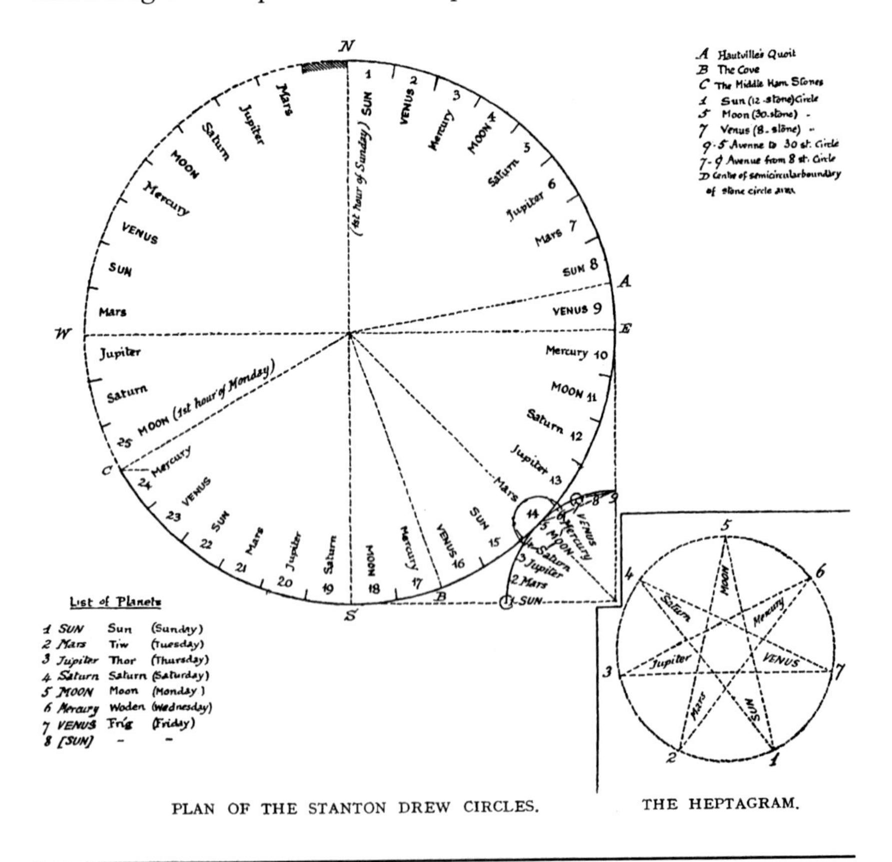

PLAN OF THE STANTON DREW CIRCLES.

THE HEPTAGRAM.

16 Ernest Sibree, *Aspects of the History of Stanton Drew* (Bristol: The Burleigh Press, 1927) p.45.

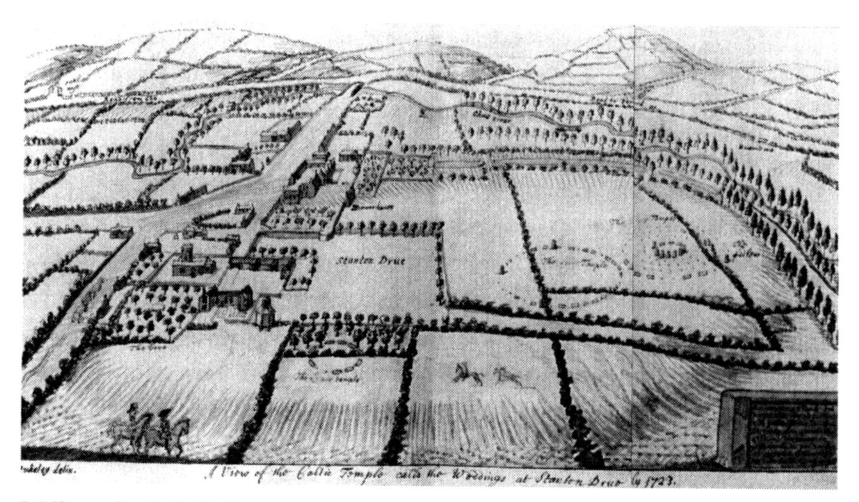

William Stukeley's illustration of Stanton Drew, 1776.

Sacred sites are best described as 'numinous' (Lat. *numen*: a deity or spirit presiding over a thing or place). A guiding principal, or the hint of a divine power, is present. Earth energies may well be made more potent as a result of rituals and invocations enacted there. A resonance between the land, the macrocosm, and its inner counterpart, the microcosm, as personified by man is a manifestation of the relations between the two.

That an awesome power resides in the Earth seems all too evident. Undoubtedly, 'Mother Earth' (Gaia) has the power to defend her territory against the rapacious and those who would seek to control her. With one toss of her luxurious tresses, all life on this planet could be ended, if she so wished. It is a sobering thought, and unfortunately, much of mankind is neither sober, nor given to a great deal of thought. Extremes of weather – tsunami, floods, and hurricanes – are perhaps an indication of an imbalance upon the planet in our times. There is a powerful lobby that insists these phenomena are caused by the action of man.

A certain Major F.A. Menzies M.C. recorded a dramatic example of the energies present at Stanton Drew. He was an engineer and surveyor who used Feng Shui and the *Chinese geomancers compass* to plot leys at megalithic sites in the first half of the twentieth century. While investigating the site he experienced an extraordinary phenomenon.

> Although the weather was dull there was no sign of a storm. Just at a moment when I was re-checking a bearing on one of the stones in that group, it was as if a powerful flash of lightning hit the stone, so the whole group was flood-lit, making them glow like molten gold in a furnace. Rooted to the spot – unable to move – I became profoundly awestruck, as dazzling radiations from above caused the whole group of stones to pulsate with energy in a way that was terrifying. Before my eyes, it seemed the stones were enveloped in a moving pillar of fire – radiating light without heat – writhing upwards towards the heavens: on the other hand it was descending in a vivid spiral effect of various shades of colour – earthward. In fact the moving, flaring lights gyrating around the stones had joined the heavens with the earth.[17]

Perhaps Mother Earth echoes the Celtic tripartite Goddess in her three aspects as the Maid, Bride and Crone. She is in this context, respectively, the Moon, the Earth and the Underworld. None can know in every aspect what transpires below the mighty oceans or beneath the mountains. Reflect for a moment upon the power of the earth as it travels through space in its orbit around the Sun. We are dwarfed by her might, yet we rarely acknowledge this simple fact. We have come to rely on artificial sources of energy, to the extent that we now cannot exist without them. Oh, what a web we weave…

Very little is known of ancient religions. The records that have been preserved are often of the practices specifically forbidden by the Christian Church. It seems likely that the ancients worshipped the sun and moon, and revered the four elements, particularly fire and water. That they paid homage to trees and rocks seems likely. The reason for this seems eminently practical. In a society where actual survival depended upon the environment, a mutual respect between man and nature seems likely. If the recognition of nature spirits increases when times are favourable, then it is likely rituals will become more intense.

Rites of propitiation naturally developed as a result of a desire to appease the natural forces of the Earth, and to give thanks for her abundance. It does not seem too great a leap in belief to personify these forces as archetypal male and female deities. The Earth Mother and the Hunter are the two entities that emerge. In later times these will

17 As related to George Sandwith, another surveyor, 16th March 1952. Major Menzies died in 1953.

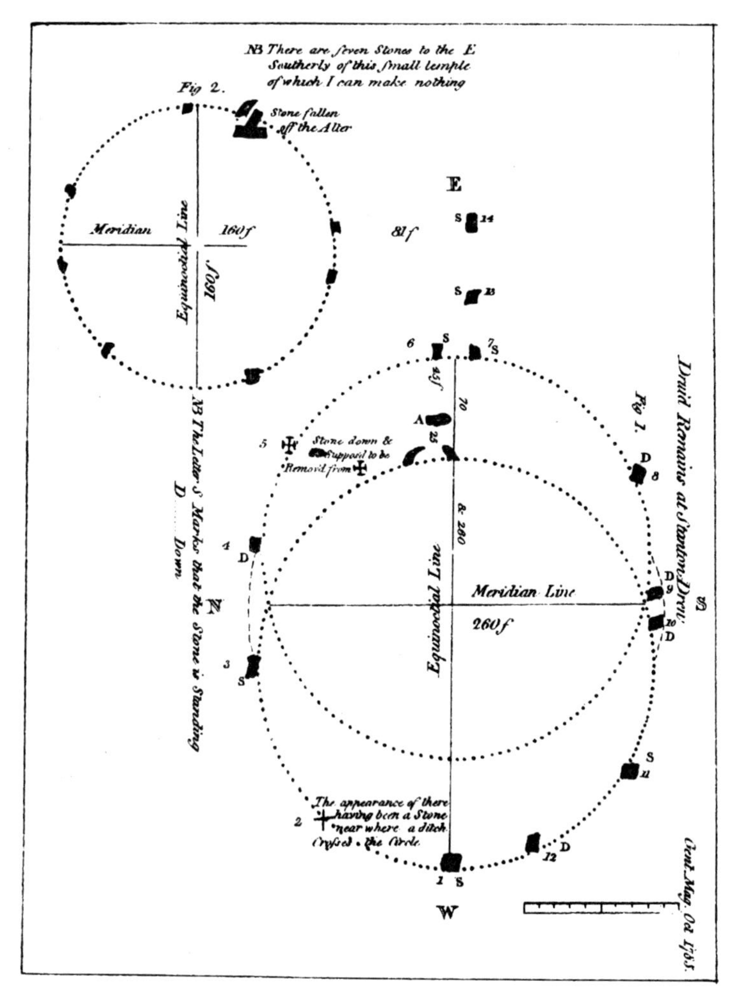

An early interpretation, published in the *Gentleman's Magazine* ***in 1785.***

become Cernunnos and the Goddess and, in a parallel tradition, Pan and Aphrodite.

In Britain, the stag held an important place in the national psyche. An animal that was hunted as well as being a symbol of male potency and strength, it features large. Cave dwellings in Somerset have revealed artefacts to support this view of the pre-Celtic culture. The female element is less overtly apparent, and here we must rely upon our knowledge of the ancients revering springs, rivers and hills.

Sacred stones appear to recharge their energies at night, and sacred sites would attract spirits and powerful entities. The word *numinous*, defined as 'mysterious' or 'awe-inspiring', is derived from L. *numen*, a deity or spirit presiding over a thing or place. A secondary meaning as 'a guiding principal' encompasses the notion of divine power. A strong 'presence' might continue to be felt as a result of the rituals and invocations enacted over the years. As Versluis suggests,

> These earth spirits are sometimes connected with the traces of human thought and emotion in a certain area. And in any case it cannot be denied that certain areas have a very real presence, intangible, but altogether recognizable. This presence is due to a resonance between geographical features, or elements of the macrocosm, and their inner counterparts in man: they are the result of a manifestation of the hidden relation between man and the world around him.[18]

That these entities exist is too well documented a phenomenon to be dismissed. It can be assumed that all ancient sites possess some 'memory' and, although some researchers insist that the energies have been depleted at certain locations, some psychic record, however elusive, is always present. The belief in the curative properties of megaliths is well documented, climbing through stone rings being the most obvious example.[19] Magnetism does have a beneficial effect on the body and it seems this therapy was known from ancient times.

18 Arthur Versluis, *The Philosophy of Magic* (London: Routledge and Kegan Paul, 1986) p.58

19 Mary English, a homeopath, made a remedy from the stones. 'Some time in the summer (2000) I took some small shards of loose stone from three of the stones' and 'by soaking in alcohol' had them made into a remedy. The twelve provers (testers) gave accounts of their experiences after taking the remedy. 'During the month of the proving, of the twelve provers, one visited Avebury, four visited Stanton Drew and one dreamt of Salisbury Plain...No-one knew what they had taken...'

4

Serpents, Dragons and the Sun

WORSHIP OF THE SUN was central to the beliefs of the Aztecs and Incas. Megaliths built to celebrate the sun's presence also exist in Egypt, Malta and England. The sun shining on a particular point at the time of the solstices is often an intrinsic feature in the design of these sites. The sun rising, astrologically, upon the back of the Lion has always been considered a symbol of great power.

Other symbols of solar power include the eagle, and the serpent. We have already discussed the Winged Globe of Egypt but not in the context of a trinity. This tripartite symbolism (Ammon, Ra and Osiris) also extends to depicting the nature of man as three separate solar bodies. The sun as spiritual, intellectual and material, is a triumvirate also analogous to the soul, the mind and the generative system of man.

At Stanton Drew it has been suggested that the Midsummer sunrise can be sighted along a line from the middle of the Great Circle to the NE circle. This actually aligns two weeks before the Solstice! But in explanation it is thought that this would give ample warning for word to be passed along that celebrations at Stanton Drew were imminent. Another alignment between the same points can apparently plot the rising of the May Day sun. The rising of the constellation Arcturus in 1620 BC and 1420 BC may also have been predicted using the same two points. My views on the likelihood of 'alignments' are expressed later.

A belief that there exists a spiritual and a physical sun was also paramount among the ancients. It was considered that the physical sun might be seen by all, but the spiritual sun was only visible to the enlightened. A scientific model of the sun suggests that in its many billions of years of existence it was once much less bright than it is today. Its surface temperature has apparently increased, and the sun grows steadily hotter. Given this, the ability to sustain terrestrial life will cease in a billion years. It is ironic that the existence of life on

Alignments have always formed a part of the mystery of Stanton Drew.

Earth is dependent upon the sun, yet that same force will eventually destroy it.

Dragons are supposed to have walked in the Garden of Eden, the first creature to appear there. Several creation myths imply that dragons brought the universe into being. In the 'Book of Formation', an ancient Qabalistic text, the Celestial Dragon commands the universe from his throne. The Chinese dragon controls all the waters of the world, and is the great ally of the gods and heroes.

Sacrifices were once left upon the top of hills to appease any dragon that made its home there. Places where it was believed a dragon lay were used as astronomical observation points. As well as high places being regarded as the abode of the gods, the placement of sighting stones and beacon fires at these points shows their importance to mortal travellers. In prehistoric times journeys were made either across ridges or along the valley floor, following river courses on foot or by water using coracles and rafts.

The dragon has always been associated with heights; Kundalini energy is known as 'raising the dragon'. The tradition of the hero doing battle with a fabulous creature has its origins in Horus fighting the vicious Seth. In other schools, Apollo subdues the Python, and Perseus defeats the Gorgon. Beowulf, as well as his campaign against Grendel, also encounters at least one unnamed dragon.

The notion of hunting and killing the dragon came with the advent of Christianity. Certain saints in the Christian canon were assigned to destroy this fabulous creature. St. Michael dispatched them at the summits of the hills and St. George made an end to those in the valleys below. Much is made of the Christian triumph in supplanting the old pagan religion, and the defeated dragon represents evil, if not Satan himself.

This orthodoxy seems to disguise a deeper truth. I would suggest that the archangel Michael, in particular, had no desire to destroy the dragon but sought to imbibe its wisdom. The Greek *spakelu* means 'to see clearly', and 'dragon' is *spakou*, hinting at far-seeing qualities. As the Chinese have always maintained, far from being a denizen of hell, the dragon is a creature of heaven. St. Michael *overcomes* the dragon in a symbolic reference to retaining the balance between light and dark. Renaissance depictions of St. Michael always include a pair of scales, and Michael's Day falls on September 24th – the Autumn Equinox – the midpoint between the longest and the shortest days.

The custom of dedicating churches to St. Michael is an acknowledgement that pagan sun gods such as Mithras had an equal status with an Archangel or even the Messiah. The church could tolerate a male god, the Sun representing a monotheistic deity, but subsequently repressed the female moon god. By the time of the Middle Ages all lunar associations were condemned as being manifestations of witchcraft.

The dragon has its origin in the *Messeh* or holy crocodile of the ancient Egyptians. Celtic kings were known as 'dragons' in the sense of *guardians*, a role assigned to the creature that protects the priceless treasures of the underworld. Uther Pendragon ('pen' means 'head') was so named because a dragon was seen in the sky at his birth. The father of Arthur thus bestows the power of wisdom upon his child. Arthur, as king, inherits wisdom from the land, of which he is guardian. The seeds of Arthur's pledge to his kingdom are sown while he is in his cradle.

When he is king, Arthur sends Yder, a young knight, to Brent Knoll, a prominent hill in Somerset. There he is given the almost hopeless task of dispatching three dragons. The knight is slain and it is rumoured that Arthur had deliberately sent him to his doom, for Yder had aroused the king's displeasure by paying court to Guinevere.

The dragon also represents fertility, the seed in the earth being brought to life by the power from the sky, a union of yin and yang. The Knights' Quest for the Grail parallels this symbiosis. Their mission, inspired by the divine, is to bring life once more to the land – the season and the time has been appointed.

Astrology appoints a sign of the zodiac to major cities and to each country. England is attributed to Aries, which in turn has a correspondence with the Dragon in the Chinese zodiac.

The dragon energy is associated with another prominent peak in the landscape, Glastonbury Tor, and can be aroused by walking the labyrinth, the sacred paths that wind about the mound. It is a Cretan spiral, the paths making continuous terraces, with vertical connections between them. Sig Lonegren, dowser and resident of Glastonbury, describes the pattern as a 'three dimensional labyrinth'.

The Vale of the White Horse at Uffington in Wiltshire is a place of great power. High on the hills, heaven and earth meet in an overwhelming majesty, and a wondrous image is inscribed in the chalk on the side of the down land hill. A combination of dragon and winged horse, this flying creature may bear its rider to the throne of the gods. A dragon shape is also made by the surrounding landscape, and *Dragon Hill* lies in the valley. This mound is probably artificial, constructed so as to receive the first rays of sunlight on the Winter Solstice. The hill makes the eye of the dragon, while the winged form is in the contours of the hills. *Wayland's Smithy*, a famed long barrow, is nearby, and these ancient ossuaries were perceived as the home of winged serpents. It is said that when Arthur returns, the White Horse will rise and dance on Dragon Hill.

Was our Antiquarian friend Stukeley aware of 'dragon paths', the ways that link the tops of mountains all over the world? This is the basis of *feng shui* which means literally 'wind and water' and 'that which can not be seen and cannot be grasped'. To create harmonious features, in accord with their system of five elements *fire, wood, earth, water, metal*, the Chinese often physically altered the landscape, as had the Egyptians before them.

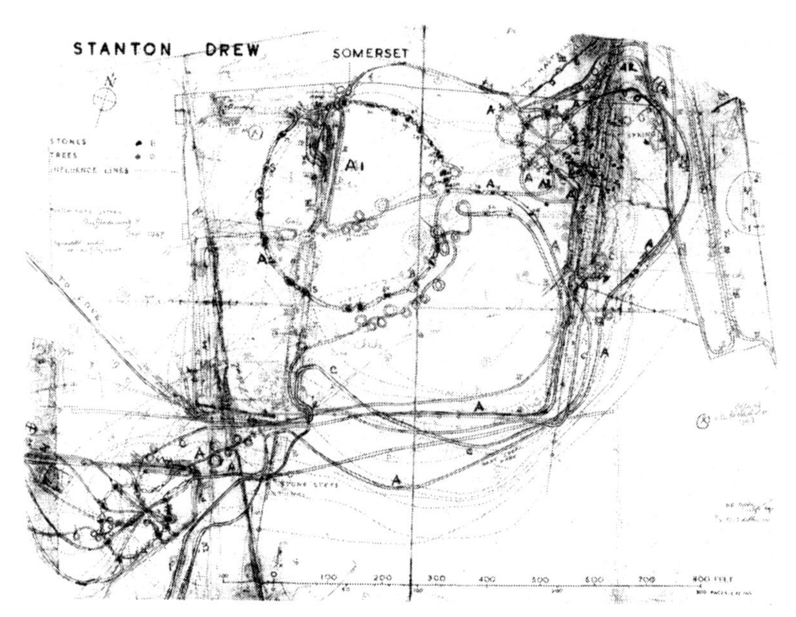

Guy Underwood's initial assessment for his dowsing survey of Stanton Drew shows many spiralling energies.

The serpent is closely connected with the dragon, the only difference being that the latter possesses wings. The notion of the serpent as protector is prevalent among many cultures. The *Wadjet* is the great serpent that protects Ancient Egypt. On Thoth's insistence a design depicting two cobras flanking a winged globe was set above the doorway of every temple. It commemorates the victory of Horus over Set. This serpent design – the *uraeus* – is seen upon the forehead of the Pharaoh, a symbol of dominion. Mucalinda the serpent king protected the Buddha while he meditated beneath the Bhodi tree. In Cambodia, serpents are still seen as the guardians of that country's temples. In Celtic culture, the car of Cerridwen, the goddess who we associate with 'The Cauldron', the forerunner of the Grail, is drawn by serpents.

The Rainbow Serpent is an important mythological creature for the Aboriginal people of Australia; it is seen as being in control of the waterholes of the desert, and preserves the precious element of water. Researcher Antony Harvey has significant knowledge of Aboriginal culture. On his visits to Stanton Drew he has experienced Serpent and Dragon energy there, similar to forces he has known in Kimberley in his native Australia.

Not all serpents are benign; the Leviathan was the 'Dragon of the sea' and Typhon, the enemy of the Olympian gods, eventually defeated by Zeus, is also many-headed. One of his children is Cerberus, the three-headed dog, with a serpentine mane and tail; he guards the entrance to the Underworld. Apollo's combat with the many-headed Hydra is commemorated in a constellation of stars.

Stukeley observed 'The Great Stone Serpent of Avebury', a monument now largely disappeared. Its avenues and circles of stones stretched for several miles across the flat Wiltshire landscape. The Serpent mound in Ohio, created by the ancestors of the Cherokee, relates to the legend of the *Uktena,* meaning 'keen-eyed'. This horned serpent has a crystal in its forehead and is associated with thunder and lightning.

Jormungandir, the Norse serpent that encircles the world represents eternity. The lemniscate, the figure of eight, seen above the head of 'The Magician' in the Tarot, and also above the female figure of 'Strength' represents eternity. The Magician also wears a coiled snake as a belt, further reinforcing his divine power and indicating the chthonic aspect of the Earth, the force associated with tunnels and secret places.

The instinctive desire is always to walk clockwise around a stone circle, in accord with the ancient warning that,

> To go against the apparent course of the sun – known before the invention of clocks as withershins or widdershins – was long considered to be unlucky and to court disaster.[20]

Each stone appears to radiate energy in bands from its centre until it touches the bands from the next stone in the circle. In the middle of the circle at most sites resides a vortex of energy. Like the coiling serpent, power is often experienced as a spiral. This contemporary Beltane chant gives the flavour of such an idea:

Spiral to the galaxy
Spiral to the shell
Spiral to the centre
Bind the lovers well.

20 Marshall p.14

This perfect form also inspired Geoff Ward to write,

> It is a divine mark on nature, what may be termed God's personal signature on the cosmos, the Great Architect's own autograph –from the cradles of stars and planets in the awesome spiral arms of galaxies to the beautiful double helix structure of the DNA molecule...[21]

The spiral may be depicted mathematically as the Fibonacci sequence in which the addition of two numbers produces the next in the sequence: 1, 2, 3, 5, 8, 13, 21, 34, 55 and so on. This desire to produce a perfectly harmonised form in the landscape is reflected in the choice of a key number upon which to base any sacred construction. In the Stanton Drew woodhenge, the pattern of nine concentric circles reflects the notion that 9 (3×3) is perfection. Labyrinths are constructed on an eightfold pattern, perhaps reflecting the number of trigrams in the *I Ching*.

To the Christian Church, the forked tongue of the serpent is seen as a sign of duplicity, thus the Bible's choosing of this creature as the tempter of Eve. Other cultures regard this dual aspect as merely a symbol of the serpent's ambivalent view of the world. In the Gnostic faith, the serpent is the depiction of Wisdom: Sophia, the female element of the Trinity. Diligence and rebirth, in the sense of enlightenment, are the qualities of the serpent.

---

21 Geoff Ward, *Spirals: the Pattern of Existence* (Glastonbury: Green Magic 2006)

5
The Watery Moon

WHY BE AN astronomer if you are a member of Neolithic society? Gazing up at the heavens cannot fail to instil a sense of the nature of existence, but it seems that our ancestors wished to represent in their immediate environment what it was they perceived beyond it. As John Dee observed,

> Thus is astrologie and astronomie carefullie and exactly married and measured in a scientific reconstruction of the heavens which shows that the ancients understode all which today the lerned know to be factes.[22]

It seems likely that stone circles functioned not only as a representation of the skies, but as a means of understanding – and later calculating – the procession of change. As Peter Marshall suggests,

> Obviously it would take many generations to observe the full cycle of the moon. Without a written language, the observations would have to be passed down either orally or in some recorded form – possibly by inscribing tallies on pieces of stone or bone or by placing wooden stakes or stones into the ground.[23]

Those who constructed the monuments were an agrarian society and thus knowledge of a planting cycle was essential to them. The times for celebration and ritual would also have been important in their lives and they would have considered how they might predict the correct occasion. Calculations involve relationships, an intellectual concept, but it is a mistake to assume that accurate measurement cannot be achieved intuitively. The methods of construction employed thousands of years ago have only been fully appreciated in recent years. Colossal monuments such as the Pyramids are 'correct' to a fraction of an inch,

---

22 Attributed to John Dee, physician and astrologer to Queen Elizabeth I.
23 Peter Marshall, *Europe's Lost Civilization* (London: Hodder Headline, 2006), p.37

and the dimensions of stone circles are also unwittingly precise. It may also be that ancient peoples were quite capable, by using sidereal knowledge, of making space-time calculations.

This desire to reflect the heavens was not restricted to European peoples. In the area that became North America were constructed 'Medicine Wheels' of wood or stones. The Big Horn Wheel in Alberta, and The Cahokia Wheel in Ohio, are both considered by modern investigators to be celestial star maps.

Robin Heath investigated the way in which our ancestors calculated the exact measurements necessary for the construction of megalithic monuments, specifically when these were employed for lunar and solar prediction.[24] He continued the investigations begun by John Michell and Alexander Thom who observed that,

> ...one thousand years before the earliest mathematicians of Classical Greece, people in these islands not only had the practical knowledge of geometry and were capable of setting out elaborate geometrical designs, but could also set out eclipses based on the Pythagorean triangles.[25]

Neolithic man could not have failed to note the lunar cycle, and he may have made an attempt to link the journey of the Sun and that of the Moon to determine the greater cycles present in the universe. It is possible that the exact position of the moon in relation to the solstices was first plotted at Stanton Drew, and the method of following the Moon's course using megaliths and sighting points was later adopted at other sites. At Stanton Drew the exact time of the Winter Solstice may have been plotted using alignments from the Cove, the Quoit being employed for this purpose at the Summer Solstice.

Over the years I have accompanied many an expert as he surveyed the site at Stanton Drew with his bevy of impressive-looking instruments. What is apparently an irrefutable scheme is then proposed, complete with immaculate calculations and impressive diagrams. In the same way I have listened politely to archaeologists as they expounded upon the reasons for the positioning of the stones, and their supposed purpose. Frankly, I have never been *entirely* convinced by any theory put to me. It is not only because these ideas often radically conflict

---

24 Robin Heath, *A Beginner's Guide to Stone Circles* (London: Hodder 1999)
25 Alexander Thom, *Megalithic Sites in Britain* (Oxford: O.U.P. 1967) p.134

but, in the case of alignments, so many of the original stones have fallen or are missing.

My own fascination with Stanton Drew lies in a more esoteric direction, but it is only correct to detail ideas that do appear to have some credence. Archaeoastronomy is a world where I do not trespass, and it must also be pointed out that the celebrated Alexander Thom came to very few conclusions about the site. I also consider it fair to include the remarks of Professor Clive Ruggles, who warns that,

> Just because a monument is aligned in a direction that we would be tempted to interpret as astronomically significant, such as the direction of sunrise or sunset on one of the solstices, this might not have been intentional.

He continues,

> The builders were not 'astronomers' in the sense that we would mean it today, but celestial objects and cycles were important to them in keeping their own lives in harmony with their world.[26]

The purpose of establishing solar alignments is to calculate the length of a solar year and thus plot a simple calendar. Lunar alignments are more marked as, at the Winter Solstice for instance, the moon is at its highest and brightest the sun at its lowest and weakest. The sun and moon set at opposite points on the horizon. At Stanton Drew the sun sets in the south-west and rises in the south-east and the moon rises in the south-east and sets in the south-west, while at the equinoxes (Mar 21st and Sept 21st) they go down at the same point. Alexander Thom conducted exhaustive experiments to discover how, with notched sticks or stones Neolithic man attempted to plot these rising and setting points.

As Robert Graves tells us, 'The Sun-god is born at mid-winter when the Sun is weakest and has attained his most southerly station…' A reassurance that the sun would return to its former power must have been sought each year, and Winter Solstice celebrations only begun when the miracle had occurred. Perhaps prompted by considerations such as these, the first 'charts' of periods of chronological time were

26 Clive Ruggles, *Astronomy in Prehistoric Britain and Ireland* (Yale University Press, 1st edition, 1999) p.86

developed. Robin Heath describes the necessary tasks that had to be undertaken.

> It must be an obvious fact that initially, for any calendar type, a set of observations had to be wrested from the skies. These observations ... had to be stretched over many years.[27]

At Stanton Drew it may be that the alignment of the Northeast Circle and Maes Knoll, directly to the north, is deliberate, as with the Round Hill to the south and Kelston to the east. Are these prominent points on the horizon sighting marks for lunar calculations? Possibly.

Many different civilizations developed their own calendar system, the Egyptians employing four different versions for instance. But the first calendars – originating from Babylon – were lunar. The Roman calendar did not become solar until Julius Caesar introduced such a system in 45 BC. The lunar calendar has to take into account the lunar month of twenty-eight days, giving thirteen lunar months. The solar system is based on multiples of two, giving us four seasons and twelve months.

Given that the site has such strong feminine qualities, the shape of each circle being ovoid is not accidental. As Alexander Thom has explained, Neolithic man was attempting, with the right-angled triangle and the circle, to (perhaps unwittingly) discover *pi*. The nearest he got was 3, which is still quite a remarkable achievement. Thus the circles are not absolutely 'true', but the circumference and radius correspond with multiples of three. From this, Alexander Thom proved the existence of the megalithic yard (2.72 ft.), a unit of calibration that is incorporated in megalithic constructions all over the world and always uniform.

This method is referred to as 'sacred geometry', a principle later used in medieval building which accounts for the deliberate 'bends' in Cathedral walls. Those who constructed these buildings were capable of erecting a wall that was true but chose to adhere to 'sacred' principles instead.

The megalithic yard is also a calculation which is in harmony with the various lunar calendars no matter how different the cycle

27 Robin Heath, John Michell, *The Measure of Albion* (Cardigan: Bluestone Press 2004) p.76

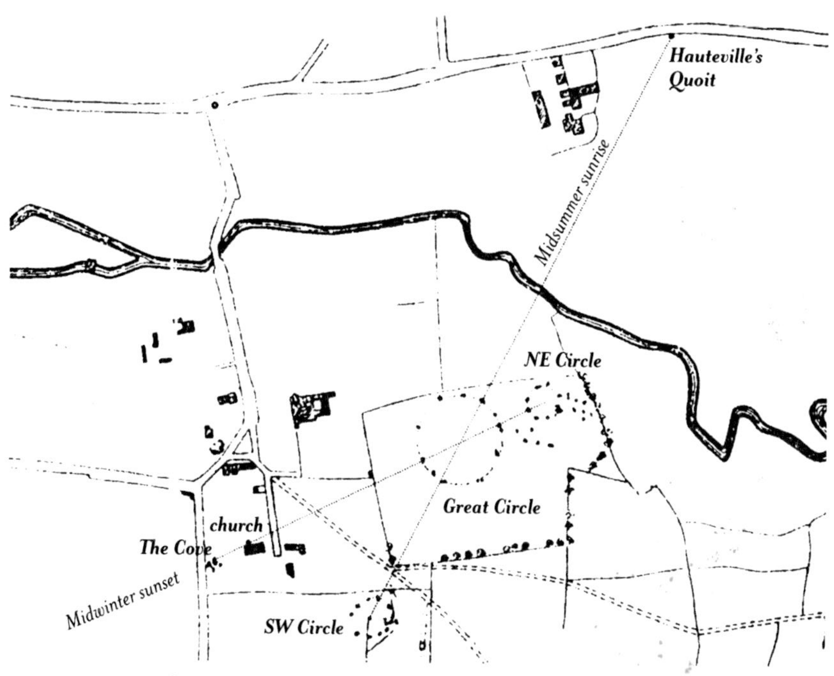

Sunrise and sunset alignments at Stanton Drew

The Northeast Circle aligns with Maes Knoll, seen here on the horizon.

of years involved. It also tallies with imperial measurements, though has absolutely no relation to the metric system. This is not surprising considering that the latter system is an artificial means of calculation having no reference to the natural world. Handy though it undoubtedly is sometimes!

Further speculation concerning lunar matters seems to be in the realms of astrology rather than astronomy. The Full Moon that occurs during the time that the Sun is in Capricorn (21st Dec – 20th Jan) will be in the opposite sign of Cancer. This is the Moon's own sign and so the emotional, watery charge is particularly potent. Stanton Drew, being so near to the River Chew, may have stronger feminine 'vibes' because of this.

During a 'lunar standstill', which occurs approximately every eighteen years, the moon can be observed close to the horizon and then subsequently markedly high in the sky. It is a dramatic moment; one that researchers believe strongly affected the consciousness of our Neolithic ancestors. The astrologer considers the Moon's effect upon us is more potent during a standstill as it is not controlled by the Sun – the feminine vibration exclusive of the masculine.[28]

Alexander Thom, who coined the term 'standstill', considered that the behaviour of the Moon during the entire year in which one occurs should also be considered. During the recent lunar standstill in 2006 the 'peaks' occurred on March 22nd, near the Spring Equinox, and September 15th, near the Autumn Equinox. It should also be noted that the sun is at its lowest point at the Winter Solstice and at its highest at the Summer Solstice.[29]

After the abandonment of stone circles as places of ritual and astronomical viewing points, the practice of observing the skies still continued in some places in Europe. The *Nebra Sky Disc* was employed in the Mittelberg Hills around 1600 BC to observe the Pleiades Cluster (The Seven Sisters) and later the Taurid Meteorite Storms, shooting stars in the constellation of Taurus. The Sun Chariot of Trundholm,

---

28 This information from Graham Ibell, an astrologer giving his views in 'Close Encounters', *The Spark* May Edition (2006) p.28.

29 This solar phenomenon may have been the reason for the construction of Stonehenge which seems to have been a "Sun Temple". The Druidic ceremonies at the Summer Solstice, and the extraordinarily large crowds who now gather there for this event, seem to confirm this.

a wheeled Scandinavian cart used for the worship of a female solar deity, was also employed for plotting eclipses of the sun.

It is interesting to note that the annual assigning of a date for the Easter festival in the Christian calendar depends upon when the Full Moon occurs.[30]

Originally honouring the goddess *Eastre* or *Eostre*, it predates the celebrations for the Sun God Mithras on December 25th. It might also be mentioned that Lent (the period from Ash Wednesday to Easter Eve) bears a strong resemblance to a fast of forty days undertaken annually in Ancient Egypt in honour of Osiris.

Dowsing to discover water that lies beneath the ground is a very old practice. Originally performed with a hazel or willow 'fork', the dowser locates a spring, or the presence of water courses. According to Sig Lonegren, dowsing 'is a bridge that can help us touch the intangible.' At Stanton Drew the presence of *primary water*, as opposed to rainwater, is a significant factor in its attribution as a sacred site. Lonegren describes the action of this water when it,

> continues its upward journey until it hits an impermeable layer of rock or clay. The pressure then forces the water out horizontally, in ... veins – cracks or fissures in the rock ... crossing veins of primary water ... when (they) reach the surface ... (they) are considered to be holy wells, places of healing, and spiritual contemplation...[31]

Dowsers may access information from the local 'morphogenetic field', a term used to describe the 'memory' of its existence that every object possesses. We may go further and speculate that our very consciousness is attuned to the nature of the universe. As Freddy Silva tells us,

> ...relationships between the geometrical forms of cymatics and the symbols of sacred geometry demonstrate that the underlying order of both the physical Universe and the nature of consciousness are not abstractions of the

30 The Table to Find Easter day, using the Golden Number, Dominical Letter and the Day of the Paschal Full Moon, is to be found in *The Book of Common Prayer*.

31 Sig Lonegren, *Spiritual Dowsing* (Glastonbury: Gothic Image 1986) p.56

> human mind but a real and structured matrix that binds everything together like God's glue.[32]

Given this, it seems logical that the stones at Stanton Drew are deliberately, or intuitively, situated above water courses. This would increase their 'power' and bestow a kind of 'static field' about them.

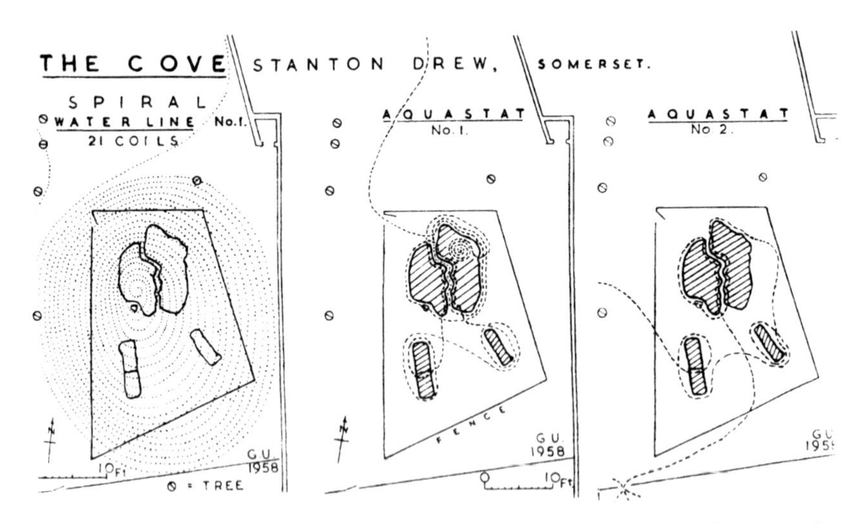

Dowsing maps by Guy Underwood, showing the location of water lines, track lines and aquastats at the Cove (above) and Hautville's Quoit (opposite page).

It is important to recognise the significance of water to the site, shown by the nearby presence of the River Chew. A tributary of the Kennet Avon, this river runs from nearby Keynsham south to Compton Dando, west through Pensford and finally to Stanton Drew. In modern times, the river narrows before flowing into the man-made Chew Lake. Springs abound locally in the hills above its course. The names Spring Farm and Watercress Farm near Dundry and Maes Knoll respectively, confirm this.

Perhaps the profusion of willows at the river's edge serves to emphasise the female energy that hovers around the site. The willow, according to Culpeper, is ruled by the Moon and is the tree of enchantment. *Wicca* and *wicker* are derived from 'willow'. According

32 Freddy Silva, *Secrets in the Fields – The Science and Mysticism of Crop Circles* (Charlottesville, VA ,USA, Hampton Roads, 2002) p.187

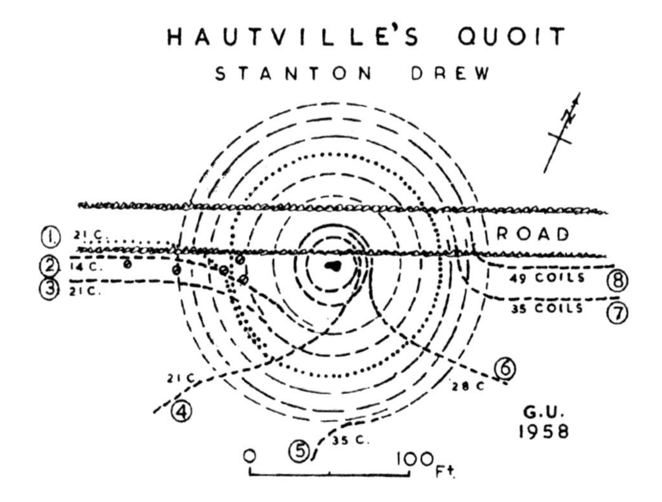

to Graves it is the fifth tree of the year and the number five is sacred to Minerva the Roman Moon goddess. The only artefacts discovered at the site are the remains of clay pots, a feminine symbol with their circular shape and function of carrying water.

Bringing together our tripartite theme of water, the Moon and female energy, it seems that to walk the paths of energy lines and follow the spiralling lines of a labyrinth increases the power there. The presence of an underground spring accounts for the 'bent' ley line between the Cove, the church of St. Mary and the NE Circle. Lonegren describes such a phenomenon,

> where the yin and yang ... primary water and the straight energy leys have come together ... reaches its peak of power at one or more times of the year ... sites are oriented towards the rising points of the Moon, Venus...[33]

The beauty of Aphrodite, her alluring presence, offering pleasure and the union of god and goddess, must be our next study.

33 Lonegren, p.89

6

The Venus Cycle

VENUS IS THE brightest heavenly body in the sky, after the sun and moon. It is certainly possible that, as well as being a lunar calendar, the stones at Stanton Drew were used to calculate the Venus cycle. The Sun and Moon were seen to be cosmic timekeepers and Sirius, Venus and Jupiter have also been employed in plotting a 365-day cycle in the heavens. The synodic interval occurs when two successive conjunctions occur between Venus and the Sun. Every 584 days Venus passes between the Earth and the Sun – five times in eight years – and her course has a connection with the solar cycle. Interesting correlations can be made between Venus cycles and the Mayan calendar.

We have examined the link between water and the mystical lunar element. It may be profitable to consider how this element relates to the cycle of gestation and birth. Rhiannon, a sensitive living in South Wales, has indicated the intimate female images she had seen in the stones. A cloaked female figure became a vulva, and another held an infant. Depictions involving a foetus and a placenta were also visible, according to her vision.

Richard Young is the owner of Stoney Close, the field at Stanton Drew where the stone circles stand. He lives in the farmhouse near the SW Circle and has shared with me some interesting anecdotes relating to the site. The fields immediately to the south of the site were known as Twinton and Furthertwinton and, as a boy, he saw cattle and sheep brought to the Great Circle at calving and lambing time. Tradition held that if this was done they were guaranteed to bear twins. It is known that animals choose to give birth over blind springs, and many abound in Stoney Close.

Mr. Young also mentioned that the field between the NE Circle and the river Chew was always wet, even after drainage pipes had been laid. No matter the season, local people used to refer to this field as 'The Waters'. A pond was once there on the route of a path, undoubtedly an energy line, from the river to the centre of the NE Circle. A rhine,[34] filled in during the 1960s, ran past the horse chestnut tree and followed the line of the fence on the East side of the field.

Colin Irving, a practising druid, owns a bungalow overlooking the site and has often seen a mist rise from 'The Waters' and cover the stones like a mushroom cloud. 'If King Arthur walked out from it I would not be surprised', he once remarked to me. Although we are aware that any Druidic link with Stanton Drew is tenuous, we do know Druids could magically create a mist so as to disappear from the sight of their enemies.

If, as is possible, the first visitors to this site were from Atlantis, a seaboard civilization, they may have felt comfortable at such a site. The Australian Aborigines speak of,

> ...jiva or guruwari, a 'seed power' deposited in the earth. In the Aboriginal view, every meaningful activity, event or life process that occurs at a particular place leaves behind a vibrational residue in the earth, as plants leave an image of themselves as seeds. The shape of the land ... echo(s) the events that brought that place into creation. ... As with a seed, the potency of an earthly location is wedded to the memory of its origin. The Aborigines call this potency the 'Dreaming' of a place...[35]

Neolithic peoples would have been aware of this feeling, surrounded as they were by a totally unspoiled landscape of hills, trees, water and the creatures that they hunted and revered. Once, an overwhelming affinity with the earth they walked upon drove those who grew crops and domesticated animals. This agrarian society developed rituals to encourage fertility. The necessary acts of ploughing, sowing of the seed, and harvesting were reflected in the celebrations at the times of the year when these tasks were undertaken. The sexual act was seen as representing all that maintained life – succour and plenty.

Folk songs reflect this earthy view of life, and most powerfully do they record and celebrate the ways of a culture and a people. These festivals and recalling of the old, simple ways are still celebrated, though perhaps in a less intense manner. The spirit is still there

---

34 A Somerset term for a drainage duct, 9' deep and 9' wide, that flows into a river. It differs from a ditch which may be blocked off at both ends.

35 Author unknown, *Dreamtime Stories of the Australian Aboriginal.*

Avenue of stones leading from the NE Circle.

however, it is shown in song and dance, and will never disappear. That desire to express the joy of living will never leave us. It begins when we are children and it is our duty to ourselves to nurture and preserve it. Human beings are tribal, often primitive creatures. The veneer of civilisation is very thin but let us, when we reveal our ancient heritage, eschew warfare and make song and dance our paean of victory.

The realisation of the menstrual cycle, the miracle of the Earth as 'the great provider' and the growing season would have prompted a reverence toward a female energy, an 'Earth Mother'. Figurines depicting this notion are very ancient and found all over the world. Performing Goddess ceremonies at appropriate times of the year was also a universal practice. Tacitus describes:

> Days of joy and feasting in all places when the goddess honours with a visit ... At those times no war is waged, no weapons are handled, the sword is sheathed. Only peace and quiet are at those times known or desired...[36]

The Roman temple dedicated to Venus in 200 AD, two miles from Stanton Drew, although far later in its construction, may still be relevant to our thesis. An octagonal structure 60' in diameter, it

36 Marshall, p.67

overlooked the River Chew and nearby was a priest's house and a holy well. The area is still known as Pagan's Hill.

Another link between nuptials and Venus has a less academic relevance to our study. The legend is told about the stones in the NE Circle once being human figures. Ostensibly they were a wedding party who were turned to stone as punishment for extending their Saturday night revels into the Sabbath. This same tale is attached to various stone circles throughout the land: the Hurlers, the Merry Maidens, the Nine Maidens and the rest.

It is possible the stones once had alternately flat and pointed tops. The custom of finishing the top of a stone wall in this manner is still common in Somerset. The style is known as 'cock and hen', a term which echoes the very distinct male and female energies that, for many visitors, emanate from the stones in the NE Circle. Tenjo, a Shingon Buddhist, is certain that the three prominent upright stones

It is possible the stones once had alternately flat and pointed tops. From a 19th Century engraving.

The author (second from left) with a party of Shingon monks at Stanton Drew.

have strong male energies and the three recumbent stones nearest the river, female. He also considers the Northeast Circle to be associated with Birth, the Great Circle with Rituals of Life, and the Southwest Circle with Death.

In Japan, the Oyu stone circle is particularly revered. Built in a style unique to that country, the site was however still used for ritual and as an astronomical calendar. I once escorted Eimei Kawakami and a party of Shingon monks around Stanton Drew, and there they performed a ritual of chanting. Eimei detected a strong female energy there, and declared the site to be a place of great compassion. He also declared that the Southwest Circle was once a place where children who had died were taken so that they might be reincarnated. Perhaps this is a portal, the place where two worlds meet – spiritual and the earthly. Death is always present where the veil is thinnest.

THIEVES

7
Comets and Energy Lines

Over the last billion years, our Earth has been pounded regularly by comets and meteors. Some of these scoured craters over a kilometre in diameter in the Earth's surface. Attempting to plot when a comet will strike the Earth is almost impossible. It is easier for science to tell us when these events occurred long ago. During the Helocene period – 10,000 years ago – our planet was hit by a comet. In more recent times, a comet struck Jupiter in 1994.

Legend has it that in the 4th Century BC a comet brought about the destruction of Atlantis and caused a reversal of the Earth's magnetic field. Shortly after this, megalithic monuments begin to appear in Northern Europe. Is it too extraordinary to conceive that Neolithic man wanted warning of future disasters? To this end, the *Book of Enoch*, the ancient Jewish religious text, gives detailed instructions on how to construct an astronomical observation device. It is in the form of a 'horizon deciclometer' or, in mores simple terms, a stone circle.

Among the survivors from the fall of Atlantis there must have been priests who were rescued by another society, one who recognized their calling. It is said that Merlin was one who was 'adopted' in this way. This select group may well have passed on their knowledge of approaching cataclysmic events, particularly the return of the comet Proto-Encke that had destroyed their land. To this end an 'early warning system' using terrestrial sites was established. These sites were located at 'power points' and mapped with the aid of a geometrical grid. In this way, temples containing records and teachings were built all over the Earth's surface.

The purpose of these sites would have been twofold, as a 'comet timetable' and as a net to harness cosmic energy. The purpose of this was to use this accumulated force in a manner we shall discuss later. By recognizing periodic increases in energy at the sites, calculations could be made and cycles of time noted. As has been explained, the notion that Neolithic man was no better than a mindless brute was still current even in the 1960s. To his credit, Professor Fred Hoyle, a leading astronomer of the time, was prepared to consider a suggestion that Stonehenge had been built as a giant computer.

> ...it demands a level of intellectual attainment orders of higher magnitude than the standard to be expected from a community of primitive farmers. A veritable Newton or Einstein must have been at work – but then why not?[37]

According to Edmund Marriage a DNA memory of another comet, one that appeared in 9000 BC, was what prompted a subsequent generation to make provisions to avert another possible global disaster. Marriage regards the intense collective effort that went into the woodhenge, and subsequently the stone circles, as giving credence to the view that,

> ...it was undoubtedly their common spiritual beliefs which enabled them to participate in the collective surges of labour that raised the great stones to the sky.[38]

Marriage believes that the purpose of constructing a megalithic monument was to provide a portal to another dimension, allowing an escape-route from this plane. Crossing the cosmic bridge into another world is part of shamanic belief, although the reason is not flight. Their cosmic journey is undertaken in order to return to the earthly plane with valuable insights. It may have been that the role of his Neolithic equivalent was to allay or transmute the great fear of natural forces that preyed upon the mind of his community. It is relevant what Versluis tells us of the weather,

> ...if one is unable to consciously affect (it), one still does so unconsciously, for as we have seen, each human being is a world in miniature and hence, when large numbers of anxious confused and disoriented people congregate in a given area, natural phenomena are disrupted just by the effect of sheer numbers of people in that state of mind. It is for this reason that the true

37 Fred Hoyle, 'Speculations on Stonehenge', *Antiquity* (1966) 40-76
38 Marshall, p.23

> magus is necessary, for the magus must counterbalance the unconscious effect upon the world of those who know not what they do, with his own conscious and compassionate harmonization of those natural forces.[39]

So the primary motive for constructing a henge would have been pragmatic, though the reasoning behind it might seem a little obscure. It is possible that the beginnings of *The Great Tao* or the *Age of Universality* began with a desire for knowledge. Might Stanton Drew have even been a Neolithic university?

Perhaps the possibility of a comet appearing and being the cause of wholesale destruction was a warning to the Neolithic peoples. Was it a demonstration by the spirits of the Earth that they had their own method of culling the population? A comet was even more dramatic than floods, drought and famine in this way.

More alarmingly in our own times, it is not only the land and its resources that have been exploited, the etheric body of the planet has also been harmed. Earth is a huge magnet because of its iron content and more accurately a dynamo. The magnetic field of the Earth may have been weakened, by at least fifty-percent, since the Industrial Revolution. The effect has been to weaken the aura, or the subtle body, that surrounds the Earth. Perhaps this may account for a diminishing of the 'sixth sense' amongst modern peoples. It seems that our 'primitive ancestors' enjoyed constant awareness, their psychic powers attuned to a high level. In our relentless technological striving we have reduced this facility and so our material gain has been to our spiritual detriment.

The result, esoterically, is that spiritual communication between gods and man, priestess and people, king and kingdom – once simply a part of existence – is harder to achieve. The ancients did not separate the secular from the spiritual, they would not have conceived it was possible to do so – to them all was one. In those times, the rapport between man and his environment was much stronger.

Since the development of technology, particularly electronic media, this symbiosis between heaven and earth, the macrocosm and the microcosm, although still existing, is less effective. Man's oneness with the universe has suffered, brought about through an obsession

---

39 Arthur Versluis, *The Philosophy of Magic* (London: Routledge and Kegan Paul, 1986) p.58

with materialism. The loss of 'synchronicity', a term that describes a dynamic particular to humanity, is also apparent. This guiding of events, in a way that may first appear to be coincidence, and later discovered to have a far-reaching causality, underlies the whole of human experience. It may govern all social, emotional and psychic interaction in the present, past, and future.

Jung, who coined the term, felt this was the conclusive evidence for the existence of the collective unconscious, a realm where communication is made via symbolism and imagery. According Jung, this state has always existed, transmitted from one generation to another. Our ancestors might not have been aware of employing symbols in magical practice; their methods of opening up the channels to the otherworld were of a more pragmatic and practical kind.

Before discussing the potent energy points to be found at Stanton Drew, it is worthwhile to consider Hamish Miller's comment that,

> Lines of Earth Energy are different to Leylines in that they are organic and weave naturally like a river. Leylines are apparently straight alignments of three or more sacred or significant sites on the surface. They are both linked to Sacred Sites, Stone Circles, Cathedrals and Churches, which are often the focus points of earth energy.[40]

Because of the earth energies present, our ancestors would have instinctively chosen to locate a sacred site at Stanton Drew. Clairvoyants Ian and Norma Parfitt detected strong energy lines on their first visit to the site, and the Bristol Dowsers group told me of 'underground rivers of energy'.

Colin Irving is only too aware of an energy line that runs from the Great Circle through the workshop in his bungalow, as electrical equipment will simply not function there. Tales of tunnels between the houses in the village are rife, along with bottomless shafts. These subterranean caverns might add to the network of energies running

---

40 Hamish Miller, Paul Broadhurst, *The Dance of the Dragon: An Odyssey into Earth Energies and Ancient Religion* (Edinburgh: Pendragon Partnership, 2000) p.178

through the site of the stone circles. Why should Stanton Drew not have the equivalent intensity of energy that is to be found at Chartres Cathedral, or even nearby Wells?

A whole network of Leys abound at Stanton Drew. A line runs from the nearby St. Mary's church – likely to have been built on a much older site – to Dolebury Camp, an Iron Age fort, and to Brean Down. Another passes through Axbridge and Brent Knoll. Yet another ley passes through the stones from the ancient settlement at Cameley, linked with the Knights Templar, on its way to Maes Knoll and then to the Market Cross in the old city centre of Bristol. Dundry Down and Cadbury Camp, the site at Tickenham, are also aligned with Stanton Drew.

The landscape of Somerset is a terrain where isolated landmarks rise dramatically above what was once flooded moors. These have historically sustained settlements, hence their significance. Flat Holm and Steep Holm, the islands in the Bristol Channel, and the hills – Crook Peak, Bleadon Hill and The Mendips – add a harmony to the scene with their essentially feminine shape. At the same time as the Stanton Drew stone circles were established, the previously mentioned Brean Down owned a sacred site. A Roman Temple, excavated in the 1960s, was built later at the same location.

Peter Marshall[41] suggests that the rafts carrying the Blue Stones, intended for the building of Stonehenge and transported from Preseli to Wiltshire by water, made a temporary halt at Steep Holm.

41 Peter Marshall, *Europe's Lost Civilization* (London: Headline, 2004)

8

Sacrificing the King

THE CYCLE OF growth and decay must occur annually to sustain the land. If this divine promise is not fulfilled, then the power of heaven to bring fertility must somehow be encouraged to return. The myths of Adonis and Attis follow this theme. Considered by Jessie L. Weston in *From Ritual to Romance* to be vegetation gods as they represent the passage of the seasons, in this context they also symbolise the rebirth of the land. Adonis is Thamuz, the Syrian Pan, who was killed by a boar when hunting. His death represents Winter killed by Spring, the return of life and thus the theme of resurrection. The Boar is assigned astrologically to Aries, and the Sun enters this sign on March 21st., the first day of Spring.

Adonis, who was loved by Aphrodite, is mourned by all women at his death; they then rejoice at his rebirth. *Adonia* was a midsummer festival celebrated in Greece with a display of flowers, particularly species known to be short-lived. Attis, by castrating himself in religious frenzy, is aligned to the Fisher King, impotent guardian of the Waste Land – depicted so definitively by T.S. Eliot – who waits for the kingdom to be restored. This will only be so when the Quest for the Holy Grail, the ultimate symbol of sustenance and plenty, is successful. Then life and fertility will return to the barren lands.

The Isle of Avalon with Glastonbury as its central focus has the greatest claim to be the home of Arthur. Caerleon in South Wales also has affinity with *Rex Quondum, Rex Futurus.* As a result of the tales of Chrétien de Troyes, Brittany, where many sacred sites are to be found, has a particular link with the Arthurian tales. But Stanton Drew shares the same county as Glastonbury and has as much claim as a place of power as does Glastonbury Tor, the Chalice Well or the Lady Chapel.

We may connect stone circles to the Round Table, for Camelot is only the continuation of an ancient theme. It is the choosing of the king, the ritual that ensures the divine power is continuous upon Earth.

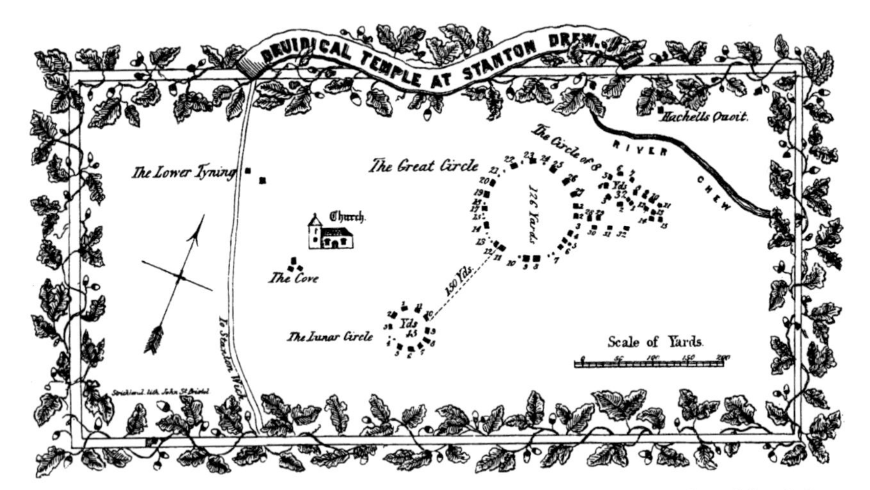

1856 map of the site as a druid temple, from a privately circulated book by George Jones, produced for members of the Mona Lodge of Ancient Druids.

'The King is dead, long live The King'. It is said that the anointing of the new monarch was made at a stone circle, and the legend of the 'sword in the stone' originated from there.

The potency of the leader of the tribe was considered of paramount importance, as it reflected the health of the land and the people themselves. Their psychic and physical well-being depended upon him, and if he became weak, then he must be ritually killed and a new king rise from the ashes of his funeral pyre.

The chief, the leader of men, was seen as divine, the deity incarnate. The ritual of 'the crowning of the king' reflects the evoking of such a spirit. As Heraclitus says, 'Gods and men live each other's lives and die each other's deaths'. The Wizard too must "sacrifice himself for others, 'giving' up the ego in order to benefit those around him."[42]

The notion of the 'warrior/sorcerer' is intriguing. It is manifest in the *modus operandi* of the Celtic warrior, one in direct contrast to the orderly ways of the Roman soldiery. Often the Celts' *laissez faire* attitude to battle was their undoing, but that was their nature. They did have one extraordinary characteristic, the ability to 'shape-shift'. The transmuting of the reasonably benign character of the Celt into an almost demonic, frenzied creature was the result of a magical act.

42 Arthur Versluis, *The Philosophy of Magic* (London: Routledge and Kegan Paul, 1986) p.90

His whole being would be subject to a mysterious force, summoned from the depths of his being, one which struck terror into his enemies and paralyzed them with fear.

This same ability to be transformed into a 'war machine' is to be found among the ancient Germans, the Irish and among the soldiery in the annals of Homer. There is no such tradition in the East; rather the opposite. The Sanskrit term *shanti* (peace, tranquility) encompasses the notion of extinguishing such angry and fevered passions and being transformed into a benign being.

The initiation into the mysteries was a practice in other parts of the world at the same time that Stanton Drew was active as a sacred site. This role played an important part in the functioning of the site. Any 'initiation' has at its heart a 'rebirth'. The old self is discarded, replaced by the new enlightened version. As Don Juan tells his pupil,

> '...you believe that you know a lot about the world, but do you? Do you really? You have only seen the acts of people. Your experiences are limited only to what people have done to you or to others. You know nothing about this mysterious unknown world.' [43]

The notion of the initiate giving up his earthly life to become divine has its origins among those deities who can be termed the sacrificial gods, the earliest being Osiris. Initiation can be likened to a ritual murder. Those who wished to partake of the Mysteries of Osiris and become united with this god's spirit meant a voluntary destruction of the self. Osiris represents the eternal soul in man. As Osiris is dismembered into forty-two pieces, reason is symbolically wrenched from feelings, flesh from the spirit. Isis, with the aid of Thoth, restored Osiris to wholeness. Likewise, the spirit and body of the initiate will subsequently act in perfect harmony. These rites are detailed in The Egyptian 'Book of the Dead'. During the initiation the soul is protected by boldly declaring the words, 'I am Osiris.' The Osirian rite was:

43 Carlos Castaneda, *Journey to Ixtlan* (London :The Bodley Head, 1972), p.257

> ...an exalted and final degree of initiation where the souls of men were not merely freed temporarily from their bodies in a condition of stimulated death, in order to prove the truth of survival after the great change, but where they were actually carried up to the loftiest spheres of being to the realm of the creator himself.[44]

Early man, pondering the inevitability of death, would have reflected upon the possibility of rebirth. Ideas have a habit of travelling across the astral airwaves and resurrection is certainly not a notion exclusive to Christianity. What is sought from rebirth is the gaining of *enlightenment*, the sloughing off of the unwanted and taking on new belief.

Sir James Frazer in his weighty tome *The Golden Bough* details tribal lore from thousands of years past, when 'ritual killings' were suffered by young males at the time of puberty. This 'death' is not a physical extinction but a loss of consciousness in order to liberate the soul for a journey to the other world where it engages astral entities in combat. As the poet Shelley wrote, 'How wonderful is Death – Death and his brother Sleep!'

Connecting with megaliths gives us a sense of the eternal round of life, to know and understand that continual change and transformation is all around us constantly. Jamie Sams, a Native-American, tells us,

> Our fear of change is at root a fear of death. Once we no longer fear death we are able to see that all changes in our lives are part of the constant cycle of death and rebirth. Each moment, as something in us dies, something else can be reborn.[45]

When we are dreaming we leave our customary conscious state far behind and enter a world where the rules of the game are different. It might be said that no real understanding of the nature of the universe is given to us until we have passed beyond the gate of death. On the soul's return after an initiation, enhancement of the earthly life is bestowed upon the indomitable traveller. Frazer refers to this basic belief in the strengthening of the soul as 'Totemism'.

---

44 E. Wallis Budge, *The Egyptian Book of the Dead, The Papyrus of Ani*, (N.Y., A&B Publishers, 1994)

45 Morton and Thomas p.317

Stukeley was convinced that Egyptian and Greek influences were present in the Somerset landscape. We have learned that Stanton Drew is a symbolic representation of Heaven upon earth – 'As above, so below.' – the macrocosm and the microcosm. Symbols have the power to communicate an entire philosophy with greater immediacy than the written or spoken word.

Antoine Count de Gebelin, a Renaissance scholar, is known to have owned a copy of the *Hieroglyphica*, reportedly a synthesis of Egyptian hieroglyphs, Greek, and Latin, which also contained references to the Qabalah and astrology. This distillation of knowledge was preserved at the temple of Hermopolis by an occult brotherhood who intended to gradually reveal to the world the secrets of Ancient Egypt. The *Hieroglyphica* was based upon the images found upon twenty-two stone tablets hidden in a temple located near the front paws of the Sphinx.

By gazing at these images it was believed the initiate could know the book of Thoth and be immediately transported into the presence of the gods. The original name for this collection of images was *nabi* (the Arabic word for wiseman) and they would eventually be transformed into the Major Arcana in the Tarot pack.

Perhaps, by telepathic means, a shaman may transmit information to initiates at other megalithic sites across the world. This may explain the similarity between belief systems within societies many thousands of miles apart. Marian Green has suggested that every shaman originated from Atlantis and this explains the unity of their beliefs. Atlantis, until its fall, was where all knowledge resided, a land greater than Egypt and predating it by several thousand years.

But now, we may imagine an initiation ceremony at Stanton Drew when the woodhenge had just been constructed. It is the night of the full moon, the one that falls nearest to the Summer Solstice. Isis has risen in the heavens, crowning this auspicious time. Vast fires are ablaze and an air of mystery and feminine energy abound. The young initiate stands at the north side of the river at the place where Hauteville's Quoit will later stand.

He is blindfolded and led by the shaman to the river's edge. They cross together in a small boat and process slowly to the entrance to the circle in the east. The guardian challenges the initiate and, if the responses satisfy him he may be allowed to pass. This ritual questioning always forms part of any magical ritual, from the Masonic ceremony to the present day Druidic rites enacted here.

Each circle is screened from the next so that the initiate must pass through a veil to gain the next stage of understanding. Aware of the decorated posts, hung with garlands, and the dancers who line the way, he follows a spiral path within each ring, getting ever closer to his goal, the centre of the circle. That he never actually reaches that point is intrinsic to the initiation for no one but the shaman, or the high priestess, is permitted to gaze upon the mystery of mysteries. But it is enough that he reaches the edge of the vortex of energy, for he still experiences the potency of Stanton Drew, and his initiation is complete.

9
A Holographic Universe?

It seems likely that 'energy lines' form a complex network all over the globe; these may even be a cause of subtle changes within us. Perhaps our predecessors were permanently in tune with these influences, and this may be another element in our modern consciousness that has been lost. As Blake says, "If the doors of perception were cleansed everything would appear as it is – infinite".

Much can be regained in our times if we embrace new ways of regarding the nature of the world, and by definition what actually is 'reality'. Stanton Drew, as other sacred sites, are centres of invisible energies. The world of quantum physics has much to offer, but before we look more closely at this extraordinary branch of science, we return briefly to the art of dowsing.

T.C. Lethbridge, born in 1901, a Director of Excavations for the Cambridge Antiquarian Society, concluded that dowsing put the practioner in touch with vibrations emanating from other dimensions. Lethbridge was a pioneer in the art of pendulum dowsing and discovered he could access the kingdom of death. In later researches he discovered that,

> It was necessary to hold the pendulum slightly to one side of the object, not above it. He decided that the pendulum must be registering a realm beyond death, another dimension, where everything was slightly displaced – as a pencil seems to be bent in a glass of water... (he made) a curious discovery about time. The pendulum refused to respond to the thought of time in our own world...we are in time so we cannot measure it.[46]

He recognized, countless other dimensions, or parallel worlds, and each:

46 Colin Wilson, *Mysteries of the Unexplained* (London: Dorling Kindersley 1999) p.48

> ...on a faster vibrational rate than our own world, and that we cannot see for the same reason that we cannot read the name of a station if the train flashes through it at sixty mile an hour.[47]

This 'vibration' was not some quality of the object itself but rather how the mind perceives it and reacts to it. He was also convinced that 'events are 'recorded on matter', which coincides with a belief that megaliths hold the energy of past events. This is certainly likely because of the nature of quartz, often present in the make-up of megaliths; we shall investigate this more fully later. Lethbridge even suggested that an '...electrical field of water, to which a dowser responds, could record emotions...' This phenomenon echoes a remarkable experiment performed at The University of Paris in 1982 by Alain Aspect who discovered that,

> ...under certain circumstances subatomic particles such as electrons are able to instantaneously communicate with each other regardless of the distance separating them ... each particle always know what the other is doing...[48]

We inevitably embrace the notion of the hologram because 'every part ... contains all the information possessed by the whole.'[49] We gain an entirely new way of understanding how the universe may be organised. Everything that exists is an extension of the same fundamental body, and the separateness of any entity is an illusion. Carlos Castaneda's Don Juan speaks of a certain quality that we possess from birth.

> 'Let's say that when every one of us is born we bring with us a little ring of power. That little ring is almost immediately put to use. So every one of us is already hooked from birth and our rings of power are joined to everyone else's. In other words, our rings of power are hooked to the *doing* of the world in order to make the world.'[50]

David Bohm suggests that, 'we view objects ... as separate from one another because we are seeing only a portion of their reality'[51]. The

47 Ibid. p.56
48 Michael Talbot, *Holographic Universe* (New York: Harper, 1982) p. 52, 53
49 Ibid. p.54
50 Carlos Castaneda, *Journey to Ixtlan* (London :The Bodley Head, 1972), p.252
51 Ibid. p.56

The quartz in the stones may enable them to hold the energy of past events.

animistic beliefs of the ancients embody this notion. The Celts held that the hunter and hunted were one[52] and '...shape-shifting into our animal natures, whether as bull, stag, horse, boar, cat, bird or fish, is a common feature of Celtic tales.'[53] The Book of Kells bears out this animistic approach to existence. In this wonderfully illuminated manuscript, men become animals, which in turn become trees, or birds become stars. This multi-layered approach to reality epitomizes the shamanic consciousness perfectly.

52 The horned god Cerne or Cernunnos – 'Lord of the Animals' – bears this out.
53 John Sharkey, *Celtic Mysteries – The Ancient Religion* (London: Thames and Hudson, 1975) p.12

The *raison d'être* of a shaman, then as now, is to travel between worlds so that the spiritual and material become one. The recognition of spirits, the sentient intelligences present in trees, stones and all 'inanimate' objects. The shaman recognises that all 'exists', every atom is alive and pulsating in harmony.

It has taken longer for science to embrace what was always known by magicians, that time and space are not constants, but projections of a deeper order. Past, present and future exist simultaneously and 'being' is just 'a cosmic storehouse of 'All That Is'.[54] Much of our acceptance of chronology and 'measurable' time can easily be seen as an illusion. Magic claims to 'change consciousness by an act of will', and a principle of quantum physics is that the ability to locate matter in a definite location depends upon the observer. It is fascinating, and also exhilarating, that science and metaphysics now almost walk hand in hand!

Karl Pribram, another scientist working in the same field as Bohm, suggests that because the brain has the ability to store an incredible number of memories in so small a space it must operate holographically. The ability to retrieve information so quickly indicates a cross-correlated system, which might also explain how the brain converts external stimuli into perceptual responses. Pribram's thesis is that a 'hard' reality is constructed when various frequencies, or types of sensory input, are sorted into conventions of understanding. We are now forced to accept that any objective reality can only be one possible version of what really 'exists' at any particular instant. It is all merely *Maya*, as Eastern philosophy has always maintained.

We all choose to interpret experience in our own subjective manner. It is interesting to speculate that the visionary, and that includes the artist and the poet, may own a greater understanding of events than any quantitative approach. Also, those who are 'psychically'[55] adept will often have a common view of any phenomena. Grof, a scientist working in the 1960s used the term 'Transpersonal experiences' to describe altered states of consciousness achieved with drugs or transcendental practices. His researches proved that it was possible to cross boundaries of time and space and that,

54 Talbot p.60
55 Telepathy being the most commonly known phenomenon.

> If the mind is actually part of a continuum, a labyrinth that is connected not only to every other mind that exists or has existed, but to every atom, organism and region in the vastness of time and space itself...[56]

If we imagine a tape that stretches all the way to the sun and back again, we obtain some idea of the capacity of our DNA for storing information. So it may be our consciousness that constructs our minds. In our day-to-day reality we perform in a very low level of consciousness, often being prepared to accept a 'reality' which is a consensus of the accepted view. 'A spade is a spade', we might say. This kind of experiential state based on sensory input probably serves us well enough in the ordinary way. It is when we wish to go deeper that we must consider other ways of regarding existence.

It might also be that our physical and mental well-being is dependent upon how we imagine ourselves to be, and to make that state actual we must strive to regain our personal power. It may be that 'magic' is not something that only certain individuals are capable of performing, it is all around us and within us. Everything is a metaphor of experience and, ultimately it is possible to have control of every event in our lives if we only knew how to do it.

All ancient sites where many people have regularly gathered, including battlefields, market places, and (naturally) places of worship, possess some 'memory'. Many of the stones used to build circles contain a certain proportion of quartz, a conductor of energy, and an intrinsic component of computers. The stones act partly as acupuncture points for earth energy, and partly as a 'battery'. The Mayans considered that crystal was a doorway into other dimensions, a means of meeting with the ancestors. Actual communication with the stones at Stanton Drew might be the result of shape-shifting, literally 'becoming' the stone in a dramatic transference of life-force.

The human body and natural quartz share a similar quality, in that they both constantly broadcast electro-magnetic signals. A symbiotic reaction may take place and 'energy information' becomes profound in the inner mind of the individual communicating with the stone.

56 Talbot p.78

Such occurrences as seeing faces within stones at sacred sites, and individuals passing through portals into other worlds – have been recorded.

Having spent Summer nights at Stanton Drew, I believe that the Moon activates the latent energy within the stones. Do the stones increase in size? Do they move about? Sing and dance? The researches of Mereaux seem to support the basis of this view. At Gavrinis, an island in South Brittany near Carnac, he detected the presence of electricity and magnetism in megalithic monuments, particularly those that contain granite or quartz. Mereaux also detected a significant increase in voltage emanating from stones with a North/South orientation, and the magnetic field around these was also very marked.

The properties of quartz are also a theme in the work of Chris Morton and Ceri Louise Thomas[57] whose research with crystal skulls is quite extraordinary. They detailed the qualities of piezo-electric silicon dioxide in the Mitchell-Hedges Crystal Skull in scientific tests conducted at the Hewlett-Packard laboratories. I spent some time with life size examples of these and experienced the sensation that the inside of my head had somehow transferred itself into one of the crystal skulls!

Consciously or not, has information been implanted in the stones at Stanton Drew? And if so, how will this be retrieved? Crystal researcher Frank Dorland believes that 'the way to extract information from a piece of natural quartz lies in some form of direct communication with the human mind.'[58] He explains,

> Natural quartz crystal has the ability to affect our own state of consciousness, to bring our own subconscious or unconscious thoughts to full conscious awareness, to boost vague intuitions and to enable us to recover forgotten knowledge from the distant past. ... the electro-magnetic energy waves we produce are received by the quartz (which) starts oscillating and amplifying these signals and rebroadcasts them ... and relays them back to us. [59]

---

57 Chris Morton and Ceri Louise Thomas, *The Mystery of the Crystal Skulls* (London:HarperCollins,1997) p.56

58 Frank Dorland, Crystal Healing (St. Paul, Minnesota: Llewellyn Publications 1988) p.123

59 Ibid. p.61

Many of the stones at Stanton Drew, like this one in the NE Circle, contain substantial amounts of quartz, including clusters of quartz crystals.

On one occasion, the reaction of a lapis-lazuli ball I had acquired and then taken to Stanton Drew was breath-taking. I held the lapis and went into deep meditation, one which quickly assumed the quality of a lucid dream. All the recumbent stones in the NE Circle proceeded to stand up and assume their original positions. Emerging from the dream-state some time later, I could not vouch for whether this had actually happened or not.

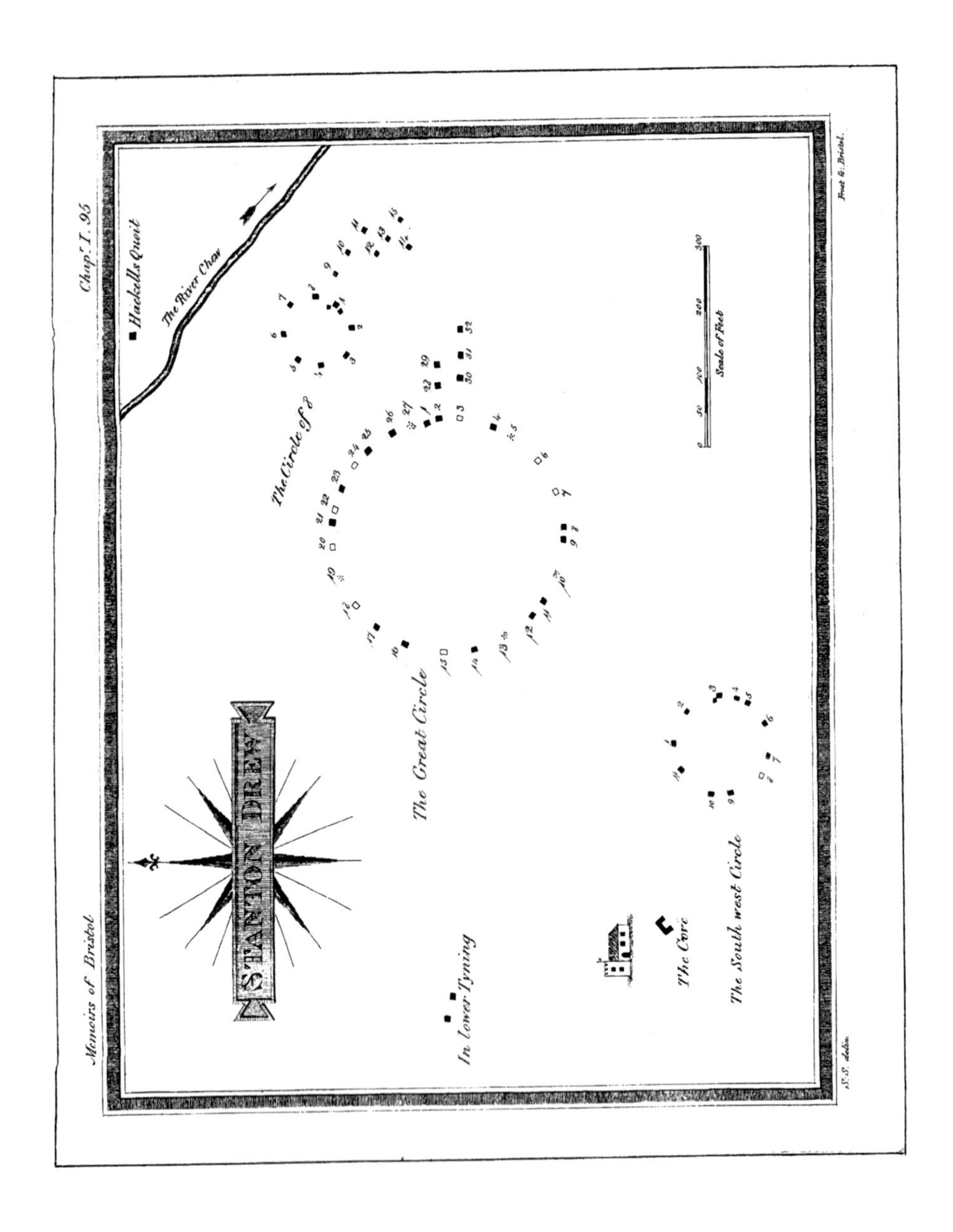

Above and following pages: a plan of Stanton Drew from Samuel Seyers' book *Memoirs of Bristol*, ***published in 1821. The numbers on the map refer to illustrations of individual stones on the plates following.***

Stones in the Northeast Circle, from *Memoirs of Bristol*, **1821.**

Stones in the Great Circle, Northeast Circle and Cove, from *Memoirs of Bristol*, ***1821.***

10
The Otherworld

THE MEANS TO gain access to other levels of consciousness are many, and all now well-documented. It is possible that those taking part in rituals may have been in a chemically induced state of consciousness. Certainly, some aspects of the shamanic tradition involve the ingesting of stimulants. The researches of J. Dronfield in 1995 and 1996 list an impressive selection of substances that he believes to have been available for this purpose in Neolithic times.

Included are ergot, deadly nightshade, henbane, fly-agaric mushrooms, marijuana and opium. Dronfield bases his thesis partly on a conviction that the carvings and designs on beaker pots in the Bronze Age could only have been produced by artists in a psychedelic state and thus a custom of using stimulants had been established for some time.

It is not beyond possibility that initiates were 'high' at ceremonies. Our contemporary equivalent is that of a music festival – 'Sex, Drugs and Rock and Roll' in once contemporary parlance. In ancient times, perhaps chanting, drumming and the wailing of pipes would provide the musical element, while mind-expanding substances would leaven the spiritual brew.

As there has never been a significant archaeological dig at Stanton Drew, no artefacts exist which would give weight to Dronfield's speculations. Did the hippy dream of 'turning on and blowing your mind' have its inception then? Certainly nearby Priddy is a popular rendezvous for those who gather 'magic mushrooms' in our own age!

In another era, Thomas Chatterton's low mood obviously did not improve when he visited Stanton Drew in the Autumn of 1769 and wrote an elegy, of which this a part.

Joyless I hail the solemn gloom
Joyless I view the pillars vast and rude
Where ere the foot of superstition trod.

Perhaps Chatterton felt the *ennui* that would accompany the approaching Industrial Revolution when the face of England would change forever.[60] The old rural ways were about to disappear and a new urban way of living become paramount. The changes that occurred in the next two hundred years will seem to be superficial compared to the changes that are about to come. Already the technological revolution makes it impossible to live one's life without being touched by it in some manner.

The 21st Century sees nature as a force that is hostile and one to be tamed and controlled. Those who know of the Goddess and respect her know that nature is a protector and a friend. The Goddess responds to whatever approach is made to her. If it is one of respect and devotion, she is bountiful, and the extent of her abundance is infinite. She wishes to give pleasure and does so eternally. If she is abused, she retires, and is cold and distant; nothing will entice her to give of herself. It is the present human condition – our separation from Heaven, our heart's desire. This is how the Waste Land first came into being.

Thus we come once more to the Isle of Avalon, an area that covers approximately four square miles, and stretches from Beckery in the west, to slightly beyond Ponter's Ball in the east. In the south, Cinnamon Lane is the boundary, and somewhere beyond St. Edmund's Hill to the north. It seems incredible that so many myths and legends could be concentrated into such a small space, but it is so. In this magical land, where once the old nature gods dwelled and perhaps the Goddess herself, it was to become in Celtic Lore the place of the dead. What place did funerary practices have in Neolithic society in Somerset?

Several long barrows were created by those who were occupying this area of Somerset, the most impressive being Stoney Littleton. A long barrow is an ossuary, the bones of the ancestors being heaped inside the earthwork in a random manner. The mound almost appears to be more significant than the actual interment. Placing bones in barrows and mounds may be attributed to a desire to hasten the soul to its resting place upon waves of earthly energy.

Unlike the later *round barrows* which are sealed and the dead elaborately laid out surrounded by their personal possessions, the

---

60 Thomas Chatterton, *The Poems of Thomas Chatterton, Miscellaneous Poems*, (London: Methuen, 1906) p.56

long barrow is an open structure. Many long barrows are found in the nearby Mendip Hills. The Fairy Toot, or *Tit* because of its mammary shape, may have been named after *Thoth* whose name was perhaps pronounced 'Tot'.

That funerary practices ever took place at Stanton Drew is extremely unlikely. Mike Pitts points out that as methods of archaeological dating change, findings at many sites are now being consigned to earlier times. It becomes more apparent that this transition took much longer than was previously supposed and the two eras may have been much more entwined.

One result of this is to blur the division between the Neolithic and Bronze Age when the practice of interment was introduced. It may have been universally adopted before the abandoning of Stanton Drew. The relevance here is that the nearest site that may have been employed for that purpose is Priddy Nine Barrows, approximately ten miles away. Often to be found in round barrows are discs of two to six inches in diameter, the significance of which is unknown. At the Nine Barrows, designs akin to stone circles are visible in the earth banks.

By the time the Romans arrived on these shores, Stonehenge was no longer used for the enactment of rituals, and its role as an astronomical calendar was also abandoned. The last significant event there was the establishing of a cenotaph over the single grave of a Bronze Age VIP. Stanton Drew also fell into disuse, the henge ditch was filled in, the woodhenge possibly burnt to the ground and some of the stones either toppled or destroyed, a very deliberate effort to signify the end of an era. Legg writes that the woodhenge was destroyed by a flash flood in 2350 BC caused by the Earth sustaining a bombardment from meteorites, but it is not possible to find any evidence to confirm this theory.

11

The Eternal Waters

As we have learned, monumental changes in weather conditions, the threat of comets and a continual sense of the presence of powerful unseen forces, may well have dominated the consciousness of Neolithic man. His belief system encompassed the notion that these forces could at least be harnessed, if not totally controlled. Mention must be made here of Newgrange in Ireland as its purpose, and its singular decorative insignia, is relevant to our thesis.

This renowned long barrow has secret chambers beneath its main construction. These are said to act as a cosmic conductor to activate and transfer energy, the same phenomenon as at the Gavrinis chamber in France. Barrows are almost invariably aligned on a North East/South East axis, the entrance pointing to the rising sun at midwinter. Their entire *raison d'etre* appears to be one of cosmic rebirth and perhaps the inviting of solar energy to gather within.

This ability is discussed by Peter Marshall who agrees with,

> ...the idea put forward by dowser Tom Graves that megalithic barrows absorb the energy from potential storms. If a site is disturbed or overloads with this energy ... a thunderstorm might break.[61]

At Newgrange, the light on the midwinter sunrise passes from the 'roof box' through the passage and into the chamber, the site being carefully oriented so that this would occur. Seen from the air, Newgrange is shaped like a *torc*, a giant representation of the cup and ring patterns often found on stone monuments. It was also known to the pagan world as *Spiral Castle*. Spirals evoke the maze and the labyrinth (from *labris* a double axe), and are symbolic of a tunnel or a pathway into the imagination.

---

61 Marshall, p.128

The placing of 'kerbstones' at the entrance to Newgrange suggests that the interior may have been used as a place of initiation and that candidates were literally hurled into a state of realisation! These stone sills are also a feature at the Gavrinis tumulus. Perhaps it should be considered that although stone circles would be suitable for calculations and utilizing geoforces, a dolmen (Cornish – *stonehole*) was specifically constructed for the latter purpose. It seems that the notion of an *enclosed* space was thought to conserve energy which could be put to some later use.

Now let us consider the engraved patterns that may be seen at Newgrange. Waves, suns, chevrons and coils are much in evidence. Vulva-like shapes also abound, echoing the shape of the stone circles at Stanton Drew. What interests us here are the spiral markings, as these are to be found on many standing stones. Legg also believed that the poles of the woodhenge were decorated or carved with spirals and curves. The spiral is a motif fundamental to the pattern of creation, as Geoff Ward explains,

> The shell of the nautilus, the tusks of elephants, warthogs and the extinct mammoths and sabre-tooth tigers, the tooth of the beaver, the claws of cats, beaks of birds and teeth of rodents, all display the same curve. So do many aspects of human anatomy, the horns of animals, the flight of birds, the volutes of waves … the curve is found in the plant world too …[62]

The cowrie shell was once considered an emblem of fertility because of its resemblance to the vulva. In Britain its equivalent is the limpet, the Cornish *brenigan* being a derivative of *bron* – breast. The ancients too knew that a physical encounter with the spiral route is a profound spiritual experience.

Spiral processional pathways probably existed at Glastonbury Tor in Somerset and at Silbury Hill in Wiltshire, examples of the sacred and spiral mountain, the symbolic World Mountains of old, *the omphalos*, where above and below, sky and underworld, were conjoined.[63]

So, is the spiral a cipher for energy? More telling, it may be a depiction of the deadly surge of a flood. A bas-relief from Nineveh

---

62 Geoff Ward, *Spirals: the Pattern of Existence* (Glastonbury: Green Magic, 2006) p.97

63 Ibid. p.99

Natural cupmarks on a recumbent stone in the Great Circle at Stanton Drew.

appears to depict figures being swept away on the tide, as do images from 2500 BC at Syros. 'The spiral image of the waves of the worried sea...'[64]

Recent geological evidence implies that the Black Sea was a fresh water lake until 5650 BC when it was inundated from the Mediterranean by a cascade four hundred times greater than the Niagara Falls. The legendary destruction of Atlantis in 1450 BC by a tidal wave, apparently the result of an eruption on the volcanic island of Thera, was punishment for the transgressions of those who inhabited this fabled kingdom. The people of Atlantis had enslaved much of the Mediterranean world and abused the magical powers bestowed on them by the gods, and this was their fate.

A fear of flooding may have prompted Neolithic man to place sacred sites on high ground away from the seacoast. Stanton Drew is relatively elevated, some distance from the Bristol Channel and protected by hills on the north side. The siting of Avebury and Stonehenge may have been due to a migration to the uplands prompted by racial memories of flooding. Bronze age trade links

64 Fernand Braudel, Roselyne de Ayala, Paule Braudel, *Memory and the Mediterranean* (New York: Alfred A. Knopf, 2001) p.78

between Britain and Greece would have meant that reports reached them, such as this from Diodorus Siculus, a Greek historian speaking of Samothrace Island, in the Aegean Sea.

> The inhabitants who had been caught by the Flood ran up to the higher regions of the island. And when the sea kept rising higher and higher, they prayed to the native gods, and since their lives were spared, to commemorate their rescue they set up boundary stones around the entire circuit of the island...[65]

At Carnac there is evidence of a half-submerged stone circle which may have replaced another when that too was engulfed by the tides at the Gulf of Morbihan. The great tumuli built in a later era may have been an attempt to protect the dead against the ocean's rise.

65 Diodorus Siculus, *The Historical Library of Diodorus the Sicilian in Fifteen Books Containing the Antiquities of Egypt, Asia, Africa, Greece, the Islands, and Europe* (Unknown, 2010)

12
A Continuing Magic

WE HAVE INVESTIGATED many aspects of Stanton Drew, and there may be more of which I am unaware. Our concluding remarks must focus upon the magical aspect of Stanton Drew, in the sense of how the site fits in with the esoteric tradition. To do this successfully we need to know some of what has gone before and be aware of how ancient beliefs are relevant to modern understanding. As we shall discover, the figure of Thoth owns much that is relevant to Megalithic sites and their nature.

It is from Sumerian, Chaldean and Babylonian society that knowledge of the mysteries originates, yet it is Egypt, a later civilization, that is generally recognized as begetting the occult tradition. When Moses led the people of Israel out of Egypt he took with him the Book of Thoth, which contained the entire Egyptian philosophy. Combined with the Qabalah, the Hebrew wisdom, this is the basis of magic.

Thoth means Truth and Time. He has the head of an ibis, a bird with a crescent shaped beak, and a human body. In another guise he is a dog-headed baboon. Cunning as a fox, he is known as *fox fire*, that phosphorescent light also known as 'will of the wisp'. In Scandinavia the Aurora Borealis is known as 'light of the fox'. Thoth invented, with the goddess Seshat, the art of writing and is the inventor of astrology and astronomy. He is also the 'great measurer' of engineering and science and is supposed to have designed and orientated the pyramids to ensure they were built according to the geometry of the human body.

He is both a solar and a lunar deity, which explains his title 'Master of the Balance'. On the one side he is the 'Voice of Ra', on the other the guardian of the moon gates having a function akin to the High Priestess of the Tarot. He helped Isis, his female counterpart, bring back Osiris from the dead, and his association with death continues in his role as consort to Maat the goddess of truth. She balances the heart of the deceased (or weighs the soul) against her feather to determine whether the subject led a pure and honest life. Thoth records their deeds and the judgment of Maat in the Book of the Dead.

Sacred to Isis are the tortoise and the turtle from which was made the body of the original lyre owned by Hermes, the Greek name for Thoth. Thus was Hermetic magic – the magic of correspondences – brought to us. Hermes owns the *caduceus* created when the god, being asked a question, caused two snakes that were fighting nearby to entwine about his staff. From that moment the caduceus was able to answer any question concerning anything in Heaven or Earth. Hermes is not only the pilgrims' guide but also the will o' the wisp, or the King of the Fairies. He still haunts dragon paths and leys and he once had his own mark in every hamlet in England.

Thoth can become a snake at will or a cat, sphinx or hawk. Set, Ra and Kheti are the deities who protect snakes, creatures that have no evil associations in Egyptian lore. Thoth is also Lugh, god of the underworld; his festival – Lugnasadh or Lammas – is celebrated on August 1st. This Celtic deity of the Arts and Sciences has, like Thoth, an exalted parentage. He is the son of Tailtiu, last queen of the Fir Bolg, the Gaelic god race before they were ousted by the Children of Danu. W.B. Yeats, the Irish poet, immersed himself in the old folk tales of his land. The eternal lines of his, 'The Lake Isle of Innisfree' reflects the city-dweller's yearning to return to the simple life.

> I will arise and go now, for always night and day
> I hear lake water lapping with low sounds by the shore;
> While I stand on the roadway, or on the pavements grey,
> I hear it in the deep heart's core.[66]

Lugh is also the god of the otherworld. He is to be found *between worlds* representing "the point between the thing and the other thing". Look for him where the mountains meet the sky, at dusk when night meets day and on the shoreline where land meets water.

The wisdom of megalithic monuments began its life as an oral lore. It was passed from one person to another, until it became part of the life of a community. Over time, its wisdom would be broadcast more widely. Much that we know has not been lost; it is simply buried in our collective psyche, ready to be recalled when necessary. The learning

66 W.B.Yeats, *Selected Poetry* (London: Macmillan, 1962) p.16

of the Druids passed into the hands of the bards, and it is from them that we owe much of our knowledge. As Lethbridge tells us:

> There is no need to go to the ends of the earth for interesting quests and excitement. It is here, anywhere in prosaic old England, at one's back door.[67]

By exclusively employing reason, we risk defining everything out of existence, so that we eventually remove all meaning from things. It is important in our lives always to continue to widen our perceptions. We may do this with a simple exercise, one that relies for its success not on a *conscious* application of the mind, rather the reverse. If we are walking, on a deserted beach perhaps, and some distance away from us we see an object that we perceive as being a snake or an alligator, then we should seek to hold that image in our mind. It is only that part of the brain responsible for rational analysis that will prevent us from continuing to embrace this image, whatever it might be. As the physical distance between us and our perceived object grows less, we might think that now we are only seeing a log, or something else quite mundane. Next we experience a point when we are seeing both the log and the creature at the same time. It is at this moment that we should bring these two senses under our control, not dismissing either of the dual perceptions, but holding them both simultaneously in our mind. I recommend doing this when the occasion arises, you will gain a great deal. You are adding to your personal store of information another way of perceiving the world, as pertinent as an 'everyday' consciousness.

Despite Stukeley's promoting of the Druids as guardians of Stonehenge, there is no direct evidence to connect the Celtic Druids with circle monuments. The legend that druids could cause megalithic stones to fly through the air remains. Perhaps such a tale is echoed in the supposed wandering ways of the Rollright Stones in Oxfordshire, and the Wimblestone in Somerset.

The modern day druids of the Dobunni Grove – the original tribe of this area – who regularly conduct ceremonies at Stanton Drew on the Celtic Quarter Days, are to be applauded for maintaining the sacred energies at the site. Stone circles are a legacy of a unique spiritual and cultural period in the British Isles. It is a wonderful and

---

67 T.C.Lethbridge, *Gogmagog: The Buried Gods* (London: Routledge & Kegan Paul, 1956) p.67

The Northeast Circle with its leaning or 'pointer' stone. It may well be that this stone was purposely placed at an angle, pointing towards the Pleiades, and hasn't simply slipped from an upright position.

The Southwest Circle. Although the stones are less impressive in stature, this small circle has an atmosphere which many people associate with healing.

uplifting experience to connect with the folk who once made this place the centre of their lives and to imagine what they did here. As Barbara Bender states,

> ...those who wish to use prehistoric sites, for worship, celebration and whatever, are perhaps being more creative than those who want to pickle the sites in aspic...[68]

After thousands of years, the stone circles of Stanton Drew still attract visitors and devotees. Long may they do so, and we can help to recharge the energies of sacred sites by performing rituals and offering prayers in these places, or by simply behaving respectfully when we visit them. In any age, man has the eternal problem of attempting to discover who he really is and I can vouch for the fact that Stanton Drew has much to teach. We may gain, with a little reflection, not only some knowledge of our ancestors, but their wisdom will be passed on to us too. That is a great gift, and one precious and eternal.

---

68 Barbara Bender, *Stonehenge, Making Space* (Oxford: Berg, 1998) p.4

STANTON DREW
STONE CIRCLE
THIS WAY

Bibliography

Aveling, Elizabeth, 'Magnetic Traces of a Giant Henge', *Nature* (390:232, 1997)

Bender, Barbara, *Stonehenge, Making Space* (Oxford: Berg 1998)

Braudel Fernand, De Ayala Roselyne, Braudel Paule, *Memory and the Mediterranean* (New York: Alfred A. Knopf 2001)

Budge, E. Wallis, *The Egyptian Book of the Dead, The Papyrus of Ani* (New York: A&B Publishers 1994)

Bull, Larry, *On Stanton Drew, Avebury and Stonehenge*, 2002 (www. bull.uwe.ac.uk)

Butler, Bill, *The Definitive Tarot* (London: Century Hutchinson 1975)

Cammell, C.R., *Aleister Crowley* (New English Library, 1951)

Castaneda, Carlos, *Journey to Ixtlan* (London :The Bodley Head, 1972)

Cavendish, Richard, *King Arthur & The Grail* (London: Weidenfeld and Nicholson, 1978)

CBA Archaeology, *Druidical Temple at Stanton Drew*, South West Issue No.1, Spring 1998

Chatterton, Thomas, *The Poems of Thomas Chatterton, Miscellaneous Poems* (London: Methuen, 1906)

Dames, Michael, *Mythic Ireland* (London: Thames & Hudson, 1992)

Dorland, Frank, *Crystal Healing* (St. Paul, Minnesota: Llewellyn Publications, 1988)

Dronfield, J., 1995 *Migraine, light and hallucinogens: the neurocognitive basis of Irish megalithic art*, Oxford Journal of Archaeology 14 261-75, 1995

Frazer, Sir James, *The Golden Bough* (Macmillan [Abridged Edition] 1949)

Grinsell, Leslie, *The Stanton Drew Stone Circles and Associated Monuments* (1995)

Hawkes, Nigel, 'Woodhenge Finds Rival Stone Circles', *The Times* (Nov. 11 1997)

Heath, Robin, *A Beginner's Guide to Stone Circles* (London: Hodder, 1999)

Hitching, Francis, *Earth Magic* (Cassell, 1976)
Hoyle, Fred, 'Speculations on Stonehenge', *Antiquity*, (1966) 40 – 76
Huntley, A.E., *The Divine Proportion* (New York: Dover, 1970)
Ibell, Graham, 'Close Encounters' *The Spark* May Edition (2006)
Knight, Gareth, *The Magical World of Charles Williams* (San Francisco: Sun Chalice Books, 2002)
Legg, Rodney, *Stanton Drew Great Western Temple* (Wincanton, Somerset: Wincanton Press 1998)
Lethbridge, T.C., *Gogmagog: The Buried Gods* (London: Routledge & Kegan Paul, 1956)
Lonegren, Sig, *Spiritual Dowsing* (Glastonbury: Gothic Image 1986)
Mann, Nicholas, *Energy Secrets of Glastonbury Tor* (Green Magic, 2004)
Marshall, Peter, *Europe's Lost Civilization* (London: Hodder Headline, 2006)
Meadows, Kenneth, *Shamanic Experience* (Dorset: Element Books, 1991)
Merze, Blanche, *Points of Cosmic Energy* (1987)
Michell, John, *The New View over Atlantis* (T & H, 2001)
Miller, Hamish; Broadhurst, Paul, *The Dance of the Dragon: An Odyssey into Earth Energies and Ancient Religion* (Edinburgh: Pendragon Partnership, 2000)
Mohan, Jean Pierre, *Les Monde de Megalithes* (Tournai: Casterman, 1989)
Morton, Chris and Ceri Louise Thomas, *The Mystery of the Crystal Skulls* (London: Harper Collins, 1997)
Pitts, Mike *Henge World* (London: Arrow, 2000)
Radice, Betty, *Who's Who in the Ancient World* (Penguin, 1971)
Richardson, Alan, *Spirits of the Stones: Visions of Sacred Britain* (London: Virgin Publishing, 2001)
Ruggles, Clive, *Ancient Astronomy: An Encyclopaedia of Cosmologies and Myth* (Yale: Yale University Press, 1999)
Sharkey, John, *Celtic Mysteries – The Ancient Religion* (London: Thames and Hudson, 1975)
Sibree, Ernest, *Aspects of the History of Stanton Drew* (Bristol: The Burleigh Press, 1927)
Siculus Diodorus, *The Historical Library of Diodorus the Sicilian in Fifteen Books Containing the Antiquities of Egypt, Asia, Africa, Greece, the Islands, and Europe* (Unknown, 2010)

Talbot, Michael, *Holographic Universe* (New York: Harper, 1982)
Thom, Alexander, *Megalithic Sites in Britain* (Oxford: OUP, 1967)
Thom, Alexander, *Megalithic Lunar Observatories,* (Oxford: OUP, 1971)
Tomberg, Valentin, *Meditations on the Tarot* (London: Element Books, 1975)
Tucker, J. Allon, 'Stanton Drew' in proceedings of the Bath Natural History and Antiquarian Field Club 5, p.257-64 (1884)
Underwood, Guy, *The Pattern of the Past* (London: Sphere, 1972)
University of Bristol Spelaeological Society Proceedings Vol II No. 1966
Versluis, Arthur, *The Philosophy of Magic* (London: Routledge and Kegan Paul, 1986)
Ward, Geoff, *Spirals: the Pattern of Existence* (Glastonbury: Green Magic, 2006)
Weston, Jessie L., *From Ritual to Romance* Cambridge University Press, 1920
Wilson, Colin, *Mysteries of the Unexplained* (London: Dorling Kindersley, 1999)
Wood, John, *A particular Description of Bath Vol.I* (1750)
Yeats, W.B., *Selected Poetry* (London: Macmillan 1962)

Lightning Source UK Ltd.
Milton Keynes UK
UKOW02f2209091114

241366UK00001B/52/P

9 781908 011589